MW01233426

Palgrave Studies in Translating and Interpreting

Series Editor

Margaret Rogers
School of Literature and Languages
University of Surrey
Guildford, UK

This series examines the crucial role which translation and interpreting in their myriad forms play at all levels of communication in today's world, from the local to the global. Whilst this role is being increasingly recognised in some quarters (for example, through European Union legislation), in others it remains controversial for economic, political and social reasons. The rapidly changing landscape of translation and interpreting practice is accompanied by equally challenging developments in their academic study, often in an interdisciplinary framework and increasingly reflecting commonalities between what were once considered to be separate disciplines. The books in this series address specific issues in both translation and interpreting with the aim not only of charting but also of shaping the discipline with respect to contemporary practice and research.

More information about this series at
http://www.palgrave.com/gp/series/14574

Kaibao Hu · Kyung Hye Kim
Editors

Corpus-based Translation and Interpreting Studies in Chinese Contexts

Present and Future

Editors
Kaibao Hu
Institute of Corpus Studies and Applications
Shanghai International Studies University
Shanghai, China

Kyung Hye Kim
School of Foreign Languages
Shanghai Jiao Tong University
Shanghai, China

Palgrave Studies in Translating and Interpreting
ISBN 978-3-030-21439-5 ISBN 978-3-030-21440-1 (eBook)
https://doi.org/10.1007/978-3-030-21440-1

This Palgrave Macmillan imprint is published by the registered company Springer Nature Switzerland AG
The registered company address is: Gewerbestrasse 11, 6330 Cham, Switzerland

Preface

This edited collection has been inspired by the need to shed light on the development of, and the current trends in, corpus-based translation and interpreting studies in the Chinese context. It has been almost 40 years since the first English corpus in China was compiled. The Jiaotong Daxue English for Science and Technology (JDEST) Corpus was developed in 1982 by the Shanghai Jiao Tong University, and it contained one million words sampled from texts written in British and American English; this was later expanded to four million words. Various types of corpora have been built since then, both by individual scholars and by institutions. For instance, the Centre for Chinese Linguistics (CCL) Diachronic Chinese Corpus, compiled by Beijing University, is the largest existing diachronic Chinese corpus in mainland China. The Beijing Language and Culture University (BLCU) Chinese Corpus (BCC),[1] developed by the BLCU in 2015, is a monolingual corpus of contemporary Chinese that covers the period from 1945 to 2015, allowing scholars to carry out a diachronic analysis.

[1]This corpus is freely available online at: http://bcc.blcu.edu.cn/ (last accessed 19 December 2016).

A number of translational corpora have also been built, encouraging scholars to identify any patterns or specific features of Chinese translations, although most are English–Chinese parallel corpora. Examples include the Diachronic Chinese–English Parallel Corpus, compiled by Beijing Foreign Studies University and Qufu Normal University in China. Some corpora feature a specific genre and Shanghai Jiao Tong University has become the spearhead in this regard, as evidenced by the English–Chinese Conference Interpreting Parallel Corpus, the English–Chinese Parallel Corpus of Shakespeare's Dramas, the Chinese–English Parallel Corpus of Contemporary Chinese Fictions, and the Chinese–English and English–Chinese News Parallel Corpus, all of which were compiled by the research team at School of Foreign Languages, Shanghai Jiao Tong University.

Apparently, corpus-based research has also been expanding its horizons from linguistic research to translation studies in China. Much corpus-based work on translation and interpreting has been carried out. A good number of books in this area of study have also been published, including the book series on corpus-based translation studies published by Shanghai Jiao Tong University Press. Although an increasing number of English articles on corpus-based translation and interpreting have been published by Chinese scholars, Chinese scholarship in this particular area remains largely unknown to English-speaking academia since they are mostly written in Chinese.

Also, because 40 years is a long time in terms of a research cycle, it is now necessary to reflect on the development of corpus-based translation and interpreting studies in the Chinese context. This book will fill this void by emphasizing perspectives emerging from an area that has traditionally been given scant consideration in English-language dominated literature. Consequently, by including the most up-to-date corpus-based research, this book, we believe, will not only receive wide scholarly attention, but will also foster and support individual and collaborative international research.

Shanghai, China

Kaibao Hu
Kyung Hye Kim

Introduction

In this volume, the term 'Chinese' is used in its broadest sense; hence, articles by Chinese scholars outside China are also included. This is important in that it enables this book to step beyond the research boundary of the geographical space. By so doing, the book places more emphasis on new perspectives on corpus-based translation and interpreting studies, such as sociology-informed approaches to translation studies that employ corpus techniques, and the attempt to combine corpus-based translation studies and cognitive translation studies.

This edited collection consists of eight carefully selected contributions by leading Chinese scholars in the area of corpus-based translation studies. Each of the four parts in this book strikes a balance between methodological or theoretical discussion on corpus-based empirical research into translation and interpreting in China, and creates a coherent theme. The chapters, however, are not limited to a mere methodological or theoretical discussion; rather, they introduce and examine a wide variety of case studies.

Part I of this volume presents an overview of the development of corpus-based research in translation studies in the Chinese context. Part I pays particular attention to issues including the validity and applicability of Chinese scholars' contributions to 'translation universals'; and the extent to which the empirical Chinese-specific studies have contributed to the understanding of specific translational features, including typical close-ended constructions, collocations, idioms, syntax, and semantic prosodies.

Chapter "Corpus-based Research on Translational Chinese" presents a critical review of the validity and applicability of previous corpus-based studies of translation universals. It argues that studies carried out to date have relied solely on European linguistic models that cannot fully explain the patterns observed in Chinese corpora, thereby limiting their analytical scope. In order to step outside this 'comfort zone', the chapter calls for the incorporation of semantics and prosody into corpus-based research on translation universals and encourages a broader interdisciplinary approach.

Chapter "The Role of Translation Played in the Evolution of Mandarin: A Corpus-based Account" looks into the factors prompting the increase in syntactic complexity specific to Mandarin Chinese in the twentieth century, employing a diachronic comparable corpus (consisting of texts originally written in Mandarin Chinese and Mandarin Chinese translations). The analysis of the load capacity and the syntactic complexity typical of two Mandarin close-ended constructions ('Preposition + Locative' and 'Demonstrative Classifier + NP') reveals that there has been growth in the complexity of the constructions in the twentieth century that coincides with the emergence of Mandarin baihua translations since the May 4th Movement (1919). It is argued that, as far as load capacity and syntactic complexity are concerned, translation has played a major role in the evolution of Mandarin Chinese; and that, considering the very small number of translational Chinese features selectively replicated in original Mandarin, the influence of a foreign language (ST) on the evolution of Mandarin is indirect and limited.

Part II of this book reviews the development of corpus-based interpreting studies (CIS). Chapter "Corpus-based Interpreting Studies in China: Overview and Prospects" offers a comprehensive and critical review of CIS in China based on a survey of interpreting corpora developed in the region and relevant journal articles published there. A number of interpreting corpora developed to date and methodologies used in the empirical interpreting studies, as well as some challenges faced by scholars in the field, are discussed. It addresses the ways in which CIS, by adopting a more holistic perspective, goes beyond mere description of data at the textual level in order to explain the discursive patterns found in the interpretation of data, thereby contributing to conceptualization of theories in interpreting studies.

Chapter "Norms and Norm-Taking in Interpreting for Chinese Government Press Conferences: A Case Study of Hedges" discusses the norms and norm-taking in interpreting and translation of Chinese political discourse as reflected in the use of hedges. Drawing on a corpus-based methodology, interpreting for Chinese government press conferences and translation of Chinese Government Work Reports are examined. It is argued that both interpreters and translators give priority to the 'faithfulness' norm in rendering hedges and explained that interpreters' performance indicates their adherence to the sociolinguistic norms of 'politeness' and 'accuracy' in interpreting, whereas the impact of other norms in translating are barely noticeable. It is also argued that the regular shifts motivated by interpreters in deploying hedges also reveal their compliance with the institutional norm of 'gatekeeping', which demands them to be loyal to the government speakers.

Part III shows how the corpus-based methodology helps researchers to investigate the translators' styles and to examine the role of semantic prosody and preference in terms of cross-language equivalence between English and Chinese. Chapter "Exploring the Roles of Semantic Prosody and Semantic Preference for Achieving Cross-Language Equivalence: A Corpus-based Contrastive Analysis of Translation Pairs in English and Chinese" discusses the role that semantic preference and semantic prosody play in achieving cross-language equivalence between English and Chinese. Analysing the recurrent word-level translation equivalents extracted from the Shanghai Jiao Tong University Parallel Corpus, the semantic preferential and prosodic profiles of the equivalents in two comparable corpora, i.e. the Modern Chinese Corpus and the British National Corpus, are investigated. It is argued that cross-language equivalence lies in co-selection patterns and that semantic prosody serves as a defining criterion for establishing pattern equivalence.

Chapter "Looking for Translators' Fingerprints: A Corpus-based Study on Chinese Translations of *Ulysses*" investigates the translator's fingerprints as manifested in their translation style. The chapter reports a case study of two Chinese translations of *Ulysses*, adopting a corpus-based approach. The parallel subcorpus of the self-built Bilingual Corpus of *Ulysses* (BCU) consists of Joyce's *Ulysses* and its two Chinese versions, produced by Xiao (1994 tran. *Ulysses*, Nanjing: Yilin Press) and Jin (1997 tran. *Ulysses*, Beijing: People's Literature Publishing House), and the comparable subcorpus includes Xiao's original writings in Chinese. The comparison of the keyword lists shows that Xiao, the literary writer and translator, leaves some traces of lexical idiosyncrasy in his composition and translation. On the syntactic level, the comparison reveals that, due to the interference of the English language, Xiao post-positions more adverbial clauses in translation than in composition, a feature that distinguishes the translated text from non-translated text. This indicates that the fingerprints of the translator are left on the translated text both as a result of their linguistic idiosyncrasy, and of the interference and constraints of the languages they are dealing with in translation.

Part IV provides critical perspectives on corpus-based translation studies in China. Chapter "Representing China in Translations of Two Korean News Outlets: A Corpus-based Discourse Analysis Approach" offers a corpus-based critical discourse analysis by looking at the ways in which China's national image is constructed in the Chinese translations of news articles provided by South Korean news outlets. Specifically, it looks at the ways in which China is portrayed in Chinese translations of the news reports on a missile deployment from two South Korean news outlets with different political and social orientations. A small corpus consisting of news reports relating to China and the missile deployment issue published in *The Chosun Ilbo*, the mainstream right-wing newspaper in South Korea, and *The Hankyoreh*, the major left-wing newspaper is designed and built specifically for this study. The stances and positions of the two newspapers towards China before and after the deployment of the missile are also examined to investigate any shifts in stance identified in the translations.

Chapter "Corpus-based Translation Studies and Translation Cognition Research: Similarity and Convergence" provides a new perspective on corpus-based translation studies by discussing what corpus-based translation studies and translation cognition research can offer to each other. The chapter discusses those two branches of translation studies, and argues that corpus-based translation studies and translation cognition research are interrelated and complementary, and will converge to give birth to a new research area of translation studies: corpus-based translation cognition research. It is argued that the use of a corpus methodology in Translation Cognition Research can help us identify the features of typical lexicons and syntactic structures that cannot be detected with the naked human eye; and that corpus-based translation cognition research thus can add to the research of CTS in areas of metaphor, cognition processes in translation, and the translator's aesthetic psychology and cultural psychology.

By critically evaluating the current research and the development of corpus-based translation studies in the Chinese context, this book provides innovative methods and valuable insights for the future of Chinese corpus-based translation studies. Both linguistic and sociological approaches to the analysis of translations are offered, while new attempts to create methodological synergy are also made by combining corpus-based methodology and translation cognition research. It is hoped that this volume contributes to the existing scholarship on corpus-based translation studies, and provides future research directions and new insights into conducting corpus-based translation studies research and other related studies.

Kaibao Hu
Kyung Hye Kim

Contents

List of Tables

The Role of Translation Played in the Evolution of Mandarin: A Corpus-based Account

Corpus-based Interpreting Studies in China: Overview and Prospects

Norms and Norm-Taking in Interpreting for Chinese Government Press Conferences: A Case Study of Hedges

Exploring the Roles of Semantic Prosody and Semantic Preference for Achieving Cross-Language Equivalence: A Corpus-based Contrastive Analysis of Translation Pairs in English and Chinese

Looking for Translators' Fingerprints: A Corpus-based Study on Chinese Translations of *Ulysses*

Representing China in Translations of Two Korean News Outlets: A Corpus-based Discourse Analysis Approach

Corpus-based Research on Translational Chinese

Corpus-based Research on Translational Chinese

Wallace Chen

1 Introduction

Corpus linguistics involves the study of natural language on the basis of authentic written or spoken data stored electronically; that is, in machine-readable form. The advent of computers in the 1950s laid the foundation for this modern view of corpora, and a corpus as we know it today may accordingly be defined as a principled collection of naturally occurring texts 'stored and processed on computer for the purposes of linguistic research' (Renouf 1987: 1). In essence, though, the text-based nature of using corpora in linguistics remains largely unchanged. What has changed dramatically after the arrival of the computer is the efficiency it offers to researchers for using and managing data. When, in the late 1920s, the Chinese scholar Heqin Chen (1928) compiled

W. Chen (✉)
Middlebury Institute of International Studies at Monterey, Monterey, CA, USA
e-mail: wallace.chen@miis.edu

K. Hu and K. H. Kim (eds.), *Corpus-based Translation and Interpreting Studies in Chinese Contexts*, Palgrave Studies in Translating and Interpreting,
https://doi.org/10.1007/978-3-030-21440-1_1

his corpus of 554,478 characters in order to generate a frequency list of Chinese vocabulary for primary education, he did so with the help of nine assistants (Huang and Li 2002: 68). It took them nearly three years of manual work to complete the list, which includes 4261 Chinese characters in use in the six text categories compiled for the corpus. Today, this pioneering work in Chinese corpus linguistics would have taken only a matter of seconds to generate on a personal computer, which can accommodate a much larger corpus with much higher levels of accuracy that has been built and processed by one researcher.

The use of authentic data is an important principle for both modern corpus linguists and researchers who used corpora prior to the arrival of the computer. Post-Bloomfieldian structural linguists such as Harris (1951) regarded a corpus as the primary source of linguistic insights. Their empirical use of large collections of recorded writings and utterances is seen as 'early corpus linguistics' in some of the literature (McEnery and Wilson 2001). Likewise, then, we could place within this broader tradition of corpus linguistics the work of a scholar such as Chen (1928), who wrote his corpus-based 語體文應用字彙 [*Applied Lexis of Vernacular Chinese*] with a pedagogical purpose in mind, asking such questions as whether elementary school pupils actually used the vocabulary they learnt.

Reusability of data (Huang 1997) is one of the major advantages of modern corpus linguistics. When corpora are stored on the computer and are (commercially) available in the form of, for example, CD-ROMs, as was the case with the *British National Corpus World Edition* released in 2000, they can be accessed by a much wider research community and facilitate various types of study based on the same data. Electronic corpora are also less prone to loss of data and to damage, a predicament that befell Chen when his second hard-copy corpus and accompanying results were ruined by fires during a Chinese civil war in the early twentieth century. In addition to data dissemination and security, reusability of corpora can also be measured in terms of their content. Corpora that were manually compiled prior to the computer era were naturally limited in terms of the data sampled and the amount of texts on paper that could be indexed at a given time. With progressively more linguistic resources becoming available today in both hard-copy and electronic versions, corpus compilers have the unprecedented advantage of being able to design very large corpora that address the limitation of data variety faced by linguists before the dawn of computer technology (Huang 1997; Leech 1991).

Drawing on the techniques and methodologies of corpus linguistics, an increasing number of scholars in corpus-based translation studies (CTS) are compiling their own databases or using existing databases to study translations from an empirical and descriptive point of view. On the other hand, CTS contributes to the study of language by building corpora of authentic translated texts that have almost never been represented in corpus linguistics (Baker 1993) during the last four decades. The now readily available corpus resources in Chinese and the relevant corpus methodology, coupled with the flow of mainstream corpus-based translation studies from the West, have largely facilitated corpus-based research on Chinese translation in the various Chinese communities. Song et al. (2013) observe that 97 articles involving corpora and translation studies were published in major Chinese journals between 1993 and 2012. Although many of these articles reported on the basics of Western corpus-based translation studies (i.e. rationale and methodology) rather than on actual empirical studies, they nevertheless successfully introduced CTS to Chinese translation researchers and practitioners. In the next section, I provide some background information on how corpus linguistics informed the study of translation (Baker 1993, 1995, 1996), and how the resulting corpus-based translation studies inspire new research agendas and the construction of translational corpora in Chinese academia. They, indeed, 'provide new tools, expand research scope and open up new paths' for Chinese translation studies (Luo et al. 2005: 56).

2 CTS and Chinese Translation Studies

Methodologically informed by corpus linguistics and first proposed in Baker (1993), CTS involves the use of electronic corpora to study translations in a systematic manner. CTS is empirical in nature and takes translated texts as its main object of enquiry. As suggested in Baker (1993: 243), translation is 'a mediated communicative event' shaped by its own goals, constraints, and context. These factors are assumed to leave their imprint on translated texts, resulting in traces or features that may be widespread and shared across different languages and cultures. Thus far, CTS scholars using large-scale corpora have identified *simplification*, *explicitation* and *normalization* (discussed in Sect. 3.3) as some of the key features of translated text (Kenny 2001; Laviosa-Braithwaite 1996; Mutesayire 2005). Other candidate features have been proposed, such as the unique items hypothesis (Tirkkonen-Condit 2002) and untypical lexical patterning (Mauranen 2000).

Some translational features are hypothesized to be inherent in cross-linguistic communication (Blum-Kulka 1986), which involves at least two languages and is thus quite different from communication in a monolingual environment. A corpus-based study by Olohan and Baker (2000), for instance, suggests that translated English tends to feature a higher percentage of reporting the use of 'that' than non-translated English. This tendency is also confirmed in the research by Frankenberg-Garcia (2002) on Portuguese–English translations. Patterns of translational features can be identified using large-scale corpora and the various methods established in corpus linguistics (Laviosa 2002; Olohan 2004). Baker (1995) suggests building three types of corpora—parallel, multilingual, and comparable (discussed in Sect. 3.3)—for the study of translations. A detailed corpus typology for translation studies is presented in Laviosa (1997), who proposes four hierarchical levels—general parameters, corpus type, language combination, and source language—as a common framework for corpus description.

Despite its established interest in the investigation of translational features for Indo-European languages (Baker 1999; Bosseaux 2001; Burnett 1999; Kenny 2000; Laviosa 1998; Munday 1998), CTS did not start to address the complexities of Asian languages until the beginning of this decade. Since the turn of the millennium, however, many Chinese translation scholars have turned their attention to CTS. Liao (2000) was the first Chinese researcher to introduce the word 语料库 *yuliaoku* [corpus] and the CTS approach to Chinese academia. Liu (2003: 25) suggested that 'translation strategies…[and]…decisions can be systematically investigated through methodologies such as corpus-based studies'. In his keynote speech at a conference in Taipei on computer-aided language learning, Sin Wai Chan (2004) of the Department of Translation, the Chinese University of Hong Kong, called for the adoption of the corpus-based approach in Chinese translation studies. The systematic methodology of CTS, along with the reusability of large-scale electronic corpora, is the high-tech vehicle with which to drive Chinese translatology into the future (Chan 2004). Individual interest has also been accompanied by institutional effort in promoting the use of corpora in translation studies, with the Dictionary and Corpus Research Center formally opened in March 2004 under the Taiwan Association of Translation and Interpretation (TATI). This exciting development in Chinese translation studies is a fruitful extension of previous corpus-based linguistic studies focusing on the retrieval of translation equivalents (Gao 1997), translation teaching (Wang 2001), and English–Chinese corpus alignment techniques (Piao 2002).

3 CTS: Offering New Research Topics in Chinese Translation Studies

As mentioned earlier, the word 语料库 *yuliaoku* [corpus] did not enter the vocabulary of Chinese translation studies until Liao's introductory paper was published in 2000. Following Baker (1995), Liao mainly introduced three types of translational corpora (i.e. parallel, multilingual and comparable) and their potential applications in translator training. He also explained to his Chinese readers how the use of electronic corpora may contribute to the study and description of translation norms and universals, which had received little attention in the Chinese academic community. This new link between authentic translational data, computer technology, and descriptive translation studies opened up a new chapter in Chinese translation studies, and has, ever since, inspired a number of small-scale corpus-based studies on new research topics that would not have been viable before the advent of electronic corpora. The following are some of the major areas in Chinese translation studies to which CTS has contributed.

3.1 One-to-One Correspondence Versus One-to-Many Correspondence

Formal equivalence has been treated as one of the 'golden rules' in the teaching of translation in Chinese communities. In Taiwan, the translation skills of high school graduates are evaluated as part of an English test administered at annual university entrance examinations. When preparing for the test (Guo 2000), Taiwanese students are advised to memorize 'standard' English equivalents for Chinese phrases, such as 在上学途中 (*zai shang xue tu zhong*) for *on one's way to school*, 被狗咬 (*bei gou yao*) for *be bitten by a dog*, and 方法之一 (*fang fa zhi yi*) for *one of the ways to do something*. Remembering these phrases is considered the key to achieving high grades (Guo 2000). Similarly, in China, free translation is recommended only when literal translation fails to convey the intended meaning, and it is estimated that, in a translation task, 70% of the sentences are rendered with one-to-one formal equivalents as the first priority (Mao 2003: 36).

This established tradition of prioritizing structural and formal correspondence has been challenged by Qin and Wang (2004). Using the *so…that* structure[1] and its translation into Chinese as an example, Qin and Wang show that, in their bi-directional English–Chinese parallel corpus, a total of 52 types of Chinese equivalents can be identified to mean *so…that*. In previous literature (Wu 2000), it was generally accepted that *so…that* can simply be, and has often been, translated literally into a causal Chinese phrase 如此 *ruci* [so]…… 以致 *yizhi* [that], whose two-part structure corresponds neatly to *so…that* both in form and meaning. In Qin and Wang's English–Chinese data consisting of literary texts, however, only 11 of the 52 Chinese equivalents of *so…that* have a two-part structure, and these 11 forms account for only 8.8% of the 248 parallel instances containing *so…that*. The remaining 41 forms are single-word equivalents of *so…that*; 31.7% of the

[1]For example: He was *so* homesick *that* he could hardly endure the misery of it (Qin and Wang 2004).

248 instances are shown to contain zero-correspondence of the English phrase. All this suggests that the conventionally accepted one-to-one correspondence between *so…that* and 如此 *ruci* [so]……以致 *yizhi* [that] has been misleading and should be replaced by a broader range of one-to-many or even one-to-zero correspondences.

For Chinese translation studies, statistics obtained by Qin and Wang are significant in that they are based on one of the first parallel English–Chinese corpora in the world. The result of this particular study challenges a long-held view of translation equivalence by offering convincing evidence on the basis of authentic corpus data. Research of this type has implications for both translation pedagogy and descriptive translation studies in the Chinese context.

3.2 Translation Techniques

Teachers of translation often collect examples of various kinds to demonstrate certain translation techniques. In his study of the English translation of a common Chinese phrase, 一……就 *yi……jiu* [as soon as], Lixin Wang (2001) manually collected 30 examples and divided them into seven categories based on the structural patterns of the English translations. Some of the English equivalents of 一……就 *yi……jiu* [as soon as] identified by Wang include *as soon as*, *immediately after*, *the moment when*, and *at the mention of*.

Wang's typology was later supplemented and expanded by Xie (2004a), who retrieved over 400 examples from a parallel corpus of six million words that he built for the purposes of contrastive linguistic study and translation teaching. Xie highlights the sheer number and wide variety of examples that a parallel corpus can offer in comparison to Wang's manual effort. He also suggests that exposing students to as many translations of 一……就 *yi……jiu* [as soon as] as possible will help them acquire a dynamic technique, which is necessary for dealing with the vast linguistic differences that exist between Chinese and English.

3.3 Some of the Studies Examining Translation Universals

Following Baker's (1993) seminal paper on the research in 'universals'[2] of translation in large electronic corpora, many Chinese scholars have attempted to carry out similar research using English–Chinese translational data. As in the study of translation universals in many European languages, explicitation is the phenomenon examined most frequently in Chinese. One of the first studies of this type is Chen (2003), who draws on a hybrid parallel/comparable corpus and identifies logical connectives as a way of realizing the phenomenon of explicitation in translated Chinese. Chen (2006), in one of the earliest doctoral dissertations on explicitation using translated Chinese in a custom-built corpus of 2.4 million words, identifies dozens of translational distinctive connectives (TDCs) that help realize explicitation in Chinese translations of English popular science texts. An integrated model of explicitation in translation is also presented in Chen (2006), which explains how explicitation is realized by a wide variety of linguistic items and what factors contribute to this phenomenon. Apart from connectives, He (2003) identifies other linguistic means that may also raise the level of explicitation in translated Chinese. These include adding lexical items and using words that are more specific than those in the source text, such as *painting board* instead of *board*. In He's corpus, the source text (*The Last Leaf* by O. Henry) contains a total of 134 sentences, of which 79 (58.96%) are shown to be made more explicit in the Chinese translation; implicitation only occurs in 13 sentences (9.7%).

Wang (2003) looks at explicitation from the perspective of text length in a comparable study. Using a bi-directional, English–Chinese parallel corpus, Wang found that both English and Chinese translations

[2]The term 'universal' has proved problematic and Baker herself is reported as suggesting that it was an unfortunate term to use in her earlier work (Mauranen and Kujamäki 2004: 2). Other more felicitous options have been suggested, such as 'regularity', 'law', or 'tendency' (Mauranen and Kujamäki 2004: 9). Several alternatives can also be considered, such as 'translation-specific feature', 'widely shared feature', 'non-language-specific feature', 'shared characteristic', or 'typical feature'.

are longer than their non-translated counterparts, and that the level of explicitation is higher in literary texts than in non-literary writings. In a parallel study, Liu (2005) observes that Chinese translations tend to be longer than their English source texts.

Shih and Shen (2004) attempt to study translation-specific features in professional and student translations of users' manuals. Their results show that simplification, explicitation, and normalization exist in both groups of Chinese translations, and that the three phenomena are more prominent in professional translations than in student translations.

In his corpus-based study on translated Chinese novels, Hu (2007) finds that, when compared with their non-translated counterparts, they demonstrate a set of translational features, including restricted lexis, repeated use of some frequency words, and a decrease in content words. According to Hu, these may be examples of simplification and normalization in translated Chinese novels, characterized by reduced lexical variety and lower lexical density.

Huang (2008) investigates explicitation represented by Chinese pronouns in parallel and comparable corpora. He concludes that a higher instance of pronouns can be found in translated Chinese than in its non-translated counterpart. Huang attributes this phenomenon to the shining-through effect (Teich 2003) of the English source texts. In their search for the Chinese 'third code' in a comparable corpus, Xiao and Dai (2010) also identify source text shining-through as the main reason behind several translational features, such as lower lexical density, more occurrence of connectives, and heavier use of passive structures. In another study by Dai and Xiao (2010), the use of more connectives is once again observable in a purpose-built English–Chinese translation corpus of parallel and comparable texts, a hybrid approach and a methodological advantage in corpus-based Chinese translation studies previously adopted in Chen (2006). Studying demonstrative pronouns (DPs) in translated Chinese versus its non-translated counterpart, Ren (2014) discovers that Chinese DPs occur more frequently in translated texts, as a consequence, again, of source-text shining through. This is a unique finding since most similar corpus-based studies in Chinese translation academia focus on personal pronouns and connectives.

Similar observations are also shown in the study by Wang and Hu (2008), who use a general, bidirectional English-Chinese parallel corpus of 30 million words to discover features and universals that may be inherent in Chinese translations. According to their study, translated Chinese shows a mixture of characteristics, including reduced lexical variety, lower lexical density, explicitation of functional words and referential pronouns, and heavier reliance on high frequency words.

Xiao (2012), in his book-length work on corpus-based study of translational Chinese, offers a comprehensive analysis of features of translated Chinese using parallel and comparable data (each having one million words). The two corpora share the same design principles and methodology, built for the sole purpose of investigating inherent features of translational Chinese as it is compared to both the available source texts and the corresponding non-translated Chinese. Another feature of the study is its focus on analysing target-language specific patterns in the translated Chinese data—for example, 被 (*bei*)-structure, 把 (*ba*)-structure, 有 (*you*)-structure, 是 (*shi*)-structure, quantifiers, aspect markers, and so on—similar to the unique-item hypotheses first proposed by Tirkkonen-Condit (2004). According to Xiao, studying these items would make it more effective to identify differences in features related to translated and non-translated Chinese.

A number of scholars have begun to explore translational features using specialized corpora. Xu and Zi (2014) investigate in a corpus of English–Chinese translation of business news a number of parameters: lexical density (LD), information load (IL), uncommon words, and distribution of parts of speech. The authors find that translated Chinese demonstrates higher LD and IL, less reliance on nouns and adjectives, increased use of verbs, and a limited set of lexical choice. A study by Zhu and Hu (2014) on semantic prosody of the Chinese *bei*-structure in translation reveals that it accepts a wider variety of verbal collocates than its non-translated counterpart. In originally written Chinese, the passive 被 *bei* [-ed] usually attracts verbs with negative connotations, such as 抢劫 *qiangjie* [rob], 偷 *tou* [steal], 开除 *kaichu* [fire], and so on. In the translated Chinese data of Zhu and Hu (2014), however, 被 *bei* [-ed] tends to attract verbs that do not have a clearly negative connotation. They conclude that Chinese translators perform their task under the influence of the effect of source text shining through to save on effort in the process of translation. Dong and Feng (2015) explore explicitation of logical connectors in scientific texts translated into Chinese. They find that the inherently explicit nature of the English source texts is transferred to the Chinese translation, making it more explicit in the use of connectors than its non-translated counterpart.

Translation-specific features are now attracting a surge of research interest in Chinese academia. All journal articles on this topic appeared from 2003 onwards, and it can be expected that more will follow this momentum into the 2020s, given the emergence of a growing number of parallel and comparable corpora online. With the methodology of corpus-based translation studies being constantly refined and standardized, we can also expect to see more interaction between Western and Eastern research groups working on the investigation of translation-specific features.

3.4 Corpus-Based Interpreting Studies

Alongside the rapid and dynamic development of CTS in Chinese academia, interpreting scholars in this part of the world began to explore the possibilities of using corpora in interpreting studies at the beginning of the twentieth century. *Breaking Ground in Corpus-Based Interpreting Studies*, Straniero et al. (2012), attempts to further establish corpus-based interpreting studies (CIS) as a sub-area of translation studies alongside CTS, both of which now form a distinctive methodology under the umbrella research paradigm of descriptive translation studies (DTS) to describe interpreted and translated languages through electronic corpora. The 'offshoot' status of CIS to CTS rendered 17 years ago in Shlesinger (1998) has now borne fruit in a coherent work describing initial findings or work in progress based on some of the first interpreting corpora in the short history of CIS. The Chinese CTS academia first turned its eye to CIS in Hu et al. (2007), which gave an overview of the discipline, and raised several issues and technical challenges moving forwards. Over the last few years, several articles (Li and Li 2010; Chen 2014) touched upon the CIS methodology and how it could enhance interpreting research and pedagogy in China. Li (2014) is one of the first CIS research projects in Chinese academia that focuses on using genuine interpreting data to study how interpreted Chinese prefabricated chunks are used in simultaneous interpreting assignments to help interpreters reduce mental processing effort and speed up delivery in a coherent and fluent manner. At the Tenth China National Conference and International Forum on Interpreting held in Xiamen, Fujian Province, in October 2014, a total of 15 CIS papers were presented. These papers cover a wide range of research topics, including corpus-based interpreting pedagogy, a study on pausing, dealing with speakers' errors, meaning units in simultaneous interpreting, compression strategy in simultaneous interpreting, lexical comparison, information processing, corpus building, and so forth. CIS is expected to develop at full throttle in the next few years in Chinese academia as progressively more interpreting scholars attempt to deal with some of the key issues on CIS; for example, technical difficulties involving corpus building (such as transcription and annotation), data representativeness, scale and scope of interpreting corpora, a clear research framework, and explanatory capabilities (Li and Li 2010; Chen 2014).

4 Major Translational Corpora in Chinese

Using electronic corpora in translation studies and pedagogy has become an attractive topic in the Chinese world since 2010. Since the first journal article introducing corpora to Chinese translation studies was published in China at the turn of the century (Liao 2000), numerous universities and academic institutions have set up state-supported projects that aim to create large-scale translation corpora of various kinds for research and pedagogical purposes. Most of these are parallel corpora; that is, collections of source texts (mostly in English) and their Chinese translations. This situation reflects the fact that source-target equivalence has always been the main focus in Chinese translation studies. The present section provides an overview of some of the major translation corpora that have been built in the Chinese world.

4.1 General Corpora

In 1992, China started its ambitious plan to create an equivalent for the British National Corpus—namely, the monolingual Modern Chinese Language Corpus (MCLC),[3] which now contains 70 million characters[4] and is considered the world's largest Chinese reference corpus. More than a decade later, in 2004, another national record was set at China's Beijing Foreign Studies University by Wang (2004b), who coordinated a state-funded effort to build the Chinese–English Parallel Corpus[5] (CEPC) that comprises 30 million words, one of the largest bilingual corpora in China. The CEPC is designed to be an 'all-purpose' parallel corpus. It is bi-directional, contains both literary and non-literary texts on various topics (some with multiple translations of the same ST), and consists of four subcorpora (translational, encyclopaedic, specialized, and bi-texts). The parallel corpus is aligned at the sentence level and tagged for part of speech. Notwithstanding the absence of spoken data, the CEPC is so comprehensively designed that it virtually offers an endless range of potential applications. These include contrastive study, translation strategies, genre study, translator style, machine translation, lexicography, translation-specific features and translator training (Ke 2002). The CEPC also contributes to Chinese descriptive translation studies by facilitating some of the first studies on translation-specific features (Ke 2005; Wang 2003). Several CEPC related projects have been proposed, including the compilation of a learners' bilingual dictionary, the creation of a national platform for translation studies and pedagogy, and the construction of CEPC-based parallel corpora of Chinese and languages other than English.

Jointly developed by the Centre for Chinese Linguistics and the Institute of Computational Linguistics (ICL) of Peking University, the Babel Chinese–English Parallel Corpus (BCEPC)[6] has been a key

[3]http://ccl.pku.edu.cn:8080/ccl_corpus/index.jsp?dir=xiandai.

[4]Roughly equal to 43.75 million words.

[5]http://www.npopss-cn.gov.cn/n/2013/0423/c362514-21241730.html.

[6]http://111.200.194.212/cqp/.

database for a series of research studies on machine translation and extraction of translation equivalents (Chang 2002, 2003; Chang et al. 2003). The corpus is on a par with the CEPC in terms of its size and design criteria. However, the BCEPC is a more ambitious project in that it is a diachronic database containing ancient and modern texts for both languages, and spoken data are included in the corpus. The BCEPC is also one of the few parallel corpora inside China that can be accessed online[7] free of charge from any Internet-enabled computer. In recent years, an ongoing project has been implemented by ICL and the Centre for Corpus Linguistics of the University of Birmingham to create the Chinese–English Translation Base (CETB). The parallel corpus is expected to contain 50–100 million words per language, and is mainly designed to facilitate research on machine(-aided) translation, lexicography, and translation practice.

The long historical relationship between China and Japan has made Japanese one of the most popular foreign languages in China next to English. Since the late 1990s, the Beijing Center for Japanese Studies has been working to create the world's first Chinese–Japanese Parallel Corpus (CJPC). Comprising 20 million characters,[8] the bi-directional CJPC mainly consists of classic novels, with a small percentage of scripts, essays, and commentaries. The corpus was completed earlier this decade and is made available in CD-ROM format with a built-in parallel concordancer.

4.2 Specialized Corpora

Whereas a clear preference can be seen in China for the construction of large-scale, general corpora of parallel texts, there is a tendency for researchers in Hong Kong to build parallel corpora that are more specialized in nature. This is a positive and encouraging move, as the potential for resource overlap is reduced. One of the most recently

---

[7]http://111.200.194.212/cqp/.

[8]Roughly equal to 12.5 million words.

announced parallel corpora in Hong Kong is METALUDE, which stands for Metaphor at Lingnan University Department of English, the world's first online interactive English–Chinese database of metaphors.[9] METALUDE consists of 9000 English metaphors and their Chinese translations. When searching the database, users are able to see the literal and metaphorical meanings of the search word, together with its grammatical information and examples of usage. Users are also allowed to interact with METALUDE by submitting new metaphors and their sources. A new proposal is under way to compile a database of Chinese metaphors to match the English database.

The increasing availability of multilingual information on the Internet has greatly benefited corpus compilers. Approved by the government of the Hong Kong Special Administrative Region (HKSAR), the Linguistic Data Consortium (LDC)[10] built and released a corpus of Hong Kong Parallel Text in 2004 using bilingual documents downloaded from the official HKSAR websites. Contained in the English–Chinese parallel corpus are three specialized subcorpora: HK Hansards, HK Laws and HK News, their respective sources being the Legislative Council, the Department of Justice, and the Information Services Department of HKSAR. The total size of the three parallel subcorpora is 108 million words, and all the bilingual texts are aligned at the sentence level. The Hong Kong Parallel Text is available from the subscription-based LDC website.

4.3 Parallel and Translation Corpora for Pedagogic Applications

Using parallel and translation corpora in translator education has become an established approach in the last decade (Wang 2004a; Zanettin et al. 2003). For trainee translators, parallel corpora provide a handy reference to translation skills and solutions, though the

[9]http://www.ln.edu.hk/lle/cwd03/lnproject/home.html.

[10]http://www.ldc.upenn.edu/.

construction of these corpora is undoubtedly a more daunting and time-consuming task than building monolingual corpora. To save time on the collection of parallel texts, some corpus builders turned to existing databases of unaligned bilingual texts. In Taiwan, a state-funded project entitled CANDLE[11] has been implemented at the National Tsing Hua University on the basis of a Chinese–English text archive of 40 million words (Liou et al. 2003). The database is a collection of bilingual articles published over three decades (1975–2002) by *Sinorama*, a monthly magazine run by Taiwan's Government Information Office (GIO) and covering a wide range of insightful reports on the island of Taiwan. Under the CANDLE project, all the *Sinorama* articles were turned into an efficient learning platform, with purpose-built tools for concordancing parallel texts, checking lexical collocations in student essays, detecting miscollocations, and improving reading comprehension. Unlike most parallel corpora that are mainly tailored for teachers to generate teaching materials, CANDLE is designed to promote active and hands-on learning by students.

There are other parallel corpora of English and Chinese that are specifically designed for the teaching of translation. At the South China Agricultural University (Deng 2005), a English–Chinese bilingual corpus of one million words has been created, its contents having been drawn from a wide variety of college-level English textbooks and their Chinese translations. Applications of this parallel corpus include the identification of multiple translations for a particular source text item, data-driven learning (DDL), generating lists of lexical items for specific student groups, providing sources of translation examples and designing corpus-based examinations. China is also home to a number of parallel corpora dedicated to specific areas, such as international relations, literary classics and computer science (Zhen and Zhang 2004).

Over the last decade, progressively more studies have tried to combine translation corpora and translator training in a more systematic approach. Wang et al. (2007) built a bi-directional parallel English–Chinese corpus to

[11]Corpora And NLP for Digital Learning of English. http://candle.cs.nthu.edu.tw/candle/index.htm.

help trainee translators reflect on the translation process and explore new skills. The authors indicate that corpus technology allows the students to become more flexible in carrying out translation assignments and to be capable of explaining translational phenomena. It also helps them rationalize their skills and construct effective translation strategies. Yang (2007) calls for an integral approach to make using translation corpora a required component in students' skill sets and in any translation curriculum. The study also suggests using parallel, comparable, reference, monitor, and online disposable corpora in conjunction with translation learners' corpora in the teaching process. This would help students systematically identify translation problems (general or specific), and facilitate autonomous learning, data-driven learning, and learning as discovery. With a corpus-based pedagogical approach, the author argues that students would be able to see advantages of corpora over conventional dictionaries, and more class activities can be designed to make full use of what translation corpora have to offer. Yang (2007) also suggests building three innovative corpora to supplement a corpus-based translation teaching approach: Chinese–English–Japanese translation corpora, corpora containing multiple translations of the same source texts, and testing archives of Chinese translation students.

Focusing on a corpus-based approach to translation assessment, Liu and Liu (2011) rely on a translation learners' corpus to evaluate students' work in the following areas: meaning accuracy, collocation, readability, lexical distribution, syntax, and translation strategy. Corpora are used here to make the translation process a thought-provoking experience, rather than simply a word conversion exercise. By adopting the Flesch Reading Ease formula, a readability test, the authors demonstrate how non-native translator trainees make their translations less readable when compared to those by native translators or authors. The former's work is characterized by longer sentences and word length, higher reliance on passive structures, preference over using heavy words, and adopting word-for-word translation and source-text syntax. In other words, translator trainees tend to transfer meaning at the word level instead of re-creating the work in another language. Liu and Liu consider the use of translation learners' corpora an effective and helpful approach to assess students' work, and to help them discover new skills and knowledge along the way.

4.4 DIY Corpora and Translation Studies

Advances in computer technology since the turn of the millennium have encouraged an unprecedented surge of corpus building around the world. In China, as in the rest of the world (e.g. in Bowker and Pearson 2002), there is an emerging trend of building specialized translational corpora for individual research projects. One of the most common applications is translator training. Using bi-texts downloaded from the Internet, over two years, Xie (2004b) built a English–Chinese parallel corpus of six million words for his own applications in several areas (e.g. TEFL, students' active learning, contrastive studies, translation teaching). The project is a good example of do-it-yourself (DIY) corpus construction, which can be achieved single-handedly using readily available tools such as Microsoft Word (for bi-text alignment), COCOA (a robust tagger), and ParaConc (for bi-text concordancing). Xie (2004b) demonstrates that a DIY parallel corpus is helpful in finding translation equivalents, studying lexical patterns across languages, and comparing various translations of the same source text.

Citing the introspective approach as a weakness in Chinese translation criticism, Xiao (2005) proposes the construction of small-scale corpora for the study of translators' styles in an objective manner. Corpora recommended by Xiao may consist of one canonical text and several of its translations, or collections of works by particular translators. Building on several papers by Baker (1993, 1995, 2000), Xiao (2005) develops a five-level schema of corpus-based Chinese translation criticism. These levels include sentence length, word frequency, distinctive lexis, theme word, and key word. Using a corpus consisting of the full text of the Chinese classic 红楼梦 *Hong Lou Meng* [*Dream of Red Chamber*] and two of its most-acclaimed English translations (the Yang and Hawkes versions), Xiao establishes for the first time that the two translations differ greatly in register. Xiao arrives at this conclusion through a comparison between the two translations' word frequencies and the Academic Word List made available by Hong Kong's Edict Virtual Language Centre.[12] Xiao found that the translation by Hawkes,

[12] http://www.edict.com.hk/textanalyser/.

a British sinologist, appears to be more typical of academic prose than Yang's version. This observation is based on the fact that there are 75 words in Hawkes' translation that are included in the Academic Word List, compared to only 30 in Yang's version. The corpus-based approach adopted by Xiao represents an innovative experiment in Chinese translation criticism and provides more convincing evidence than previous studies based on a few randomly selected examples.

A similar approach is also proposed by Jiang (2005), who stresses the potential of using parallel corpora to study register and style in legal translation. Applications of corpora to forensic linguistics include such areas as lexicography, semantics, syntax, discourse analysis, legal translation, and the teaching of legal English. Jiang finds it particularly useful to adopt the corpus-based approach for the study of translators' style, gender difference in language use, and the linguistic patterning of legal translations.

Another interesting DIY project can be found in Tan (2015), who studies annotations in Chinese subtitling of the Fox TV series *Prison Break*. The author looks at how annotations are used in translating cultural terms, puns, rare items, non-verbal screen messages, and foreign language conversations in subtitles from English into Chinese. The conclusions drawn indicate that Chinese translators, when faced with these challenges in subtitling, tend to provide a literal translation followed by an added annotation in parentheses. According to the author, this strategy is to ensure faithfulness, accuracy, and, at the same time, audience understanding.

5 Future Directions

The thriving development of CTS and CIS in Chinese academia since the turn of the millennium has been remarkable, with many positive signs that this trend will continue into the future. For example, there has been a conference on CTS or CIS almost every year since the late 2000s, the latest being the Third National Conference on Corpus-based Translation Studies held at University of South China in November 2015. Also, there is a book series on CTS/CIS, comprising four volumes so far, published by Shanghai Jiao Tong University Press.

The same institution is also home to an annual week-long summer school on CTS/CIS research methodology launched in 2012. A thematic strand on CTS/CIS can be seen in almost every major conference on translation or interpretation in Chinese academia, for instance, the Tenth China National Conference and International Forum on Interpreting held at Xiamen University in October 2014. It is now relatively easy to find one or more active researchers on CTS/CIS in almost every language-related department in China's major universities.

With these encouraging developments, an abundant array of published studies on CTS, and numerous research resources allocated in this area since the late 1990s, it can be confidently said that CTS has firmly established itself as a major discipline in humanities in Chinese academia. Of course, there are challenges lying ahead for Chinese CTS researchers, including the limited scope of currently available corpora, insufficient interdisciplinary collaboration, heavier focus on quantitative research and universals, scattered corpus building efforts, lack of deep-layer annotation schemes, insufficient studies on CIS, developing a CTS/CIS-based curriculum for translator and interpreter training, and defining roles of the source text in CTS (Long 2012; Song et al. 2013; Wei and Li 2013).

In a world of instant and multilingual communication across national boundaries via social media on smartphones and tablets, corpus resources of translated and interpreted materials are readily at our disposal. An interesting or inspiring lecture on Ted Talk (www.ted.com) is often translated and subtitled into many languages at the same time by volunteer translators around the world, usually completed and available online in a matter of several days. A message on Facebook or Instagram can be translated into any language at the click of a button. Students can now comfortably and effectively browse through any conceivable topic on the constantly updated Wikipedia pages in multiple languages. Imagine how these texts can be put to use in CTS/CIS research if they are collected and shared immediately online! This is what Bendazzoli (2014) calls 'CIS in the Web 2.0 Era', where all the interpreting materials are collected and shared on the Internet in an online collaborative project aimed at interpreter training or professional practice. In Bendazzoli's terms, 'collaborative' means giving back language resources and is a 'social' good that benefits us all, whether in terms of research, pedagogy, or professional use.

After 15 years of academic endeavors since Liao (2000) introduced corpora and translation studies into Chinese academia, CTS researchers in the Chinese world have examined, verified and confirmed most of the translational features and universals previously explored in Western literature. What is needed now would be a concerted effort by the East and the West to craft a shared CTS framework that 1) explains the patterns identified in a corpus in the social, political, and cultural contexts rather than simply describing translational phenomena (Huang and Wang 2011), 2) places more emphasis on the study of translation processes and on defining the representativeness of DIY corpora (Zhang and Hu 2011), 3) explores translation constraints and how translation interacts with the target language (Huang and Wang 2011), 4) investigates individual distinctiveness and creativity alongside current efforts on studying universals (Hu and Mao 2012), 5) compares different corpora to refine existing theories on translation universals (Huang & Zhu 2012), 6) examines and explains universals from cognitive, social, and contextual perspectives (Hu and Zeng 2011; Long 2012), 7) creates a wide variety of translation and interpreting corpora to include more language pairs and less-studied translated texts in the areas of politics, law, business, news reports, etc. (Long 2012), 8) identifies more translational features related to a universal (Ren 2014), 9) encourages cross-linguistic and cross-institutional collaboration on corpus building and investigation, 10) applies CTS findings to translator and interpreter education, 11) develops multimodal corpora that can be employed in the analysis of subtitling and interpreting, and, last but not least, 12) designs a corpus-based approach to the analysis of SMS texts such as Weibo and Weixin.

References

Baker, M. (1993). Corpus Linguistics and Translation Studies: Implications and Applications. In M. Baker, G. Francis, & E. Tognini-Bonelli (Eds.), *Text and Technology: In Honour of John Sinclair* (pp. 233–250). Amsterdam and Philadelphia: John Benjamins.

Baker, M. (1995). Corpora in Translation Studies: An Overview and Some Suggestions for Future Research. *Target, 7*(2), 223–243.

Baker, M. (1996). Corpus-Based Translation Studies: The Challenges That Lie Ahead. In H. Somers (Ed.), *Terminology, LSP and Translation* (pp. 175–186). Amsterdam: John Benjamins.

Baker, M. (1999). The Role of Corpora in Investigating the Linguistic Behaviour of Professional Translators. *International Journal of Corpus Linguistics, 4*(2), 281–298.

Baker, M. (2000). Towards a Methodology for Investigating the Style of a Literary Translator. *Target, 12*(2), 241–266.

Bendazzoli, C. (2014). *Corpus-Based Interpreting Studies (CIS) in the Web 2.0 Era*. Invited Talk as Keynote Speaker at the Tenth China National Conference and International Forum on Interpreting Studies: The Way Forward, University of Xiamen, China.

Blum-Kulka, S. (1986). Shifts of Cohesion and Coherence in Translation. In J. House & S. Blum-Kulka (Eds.), *Interlingual and Intercultural Communication: Discourse and Cognition in Translation and Second Language Acquisition Studies* (pp. 17–35). Tubingen: Gunter Narr.

Bosseaux, C. (2001). A Study of the Translator's Voice and Style in the French Translations of Virginia Woolf's. *The Waves: CTIS Occasional Papers, 1*, 55–75.

Bowker, L., & Pearson, J. (2002). *Working with Specialized Language: A Practical Guide to Using Corpora*. London and New York: Routledge.

Burnett, S. (1999). *A Corpus-Based Study of Translational English*. Manchester: UMIST.

Chan, S. W. (2004). *Translating for the Future: Reflections on Making a Dictionary of Translation Technology*. Paper Presented at the Conference and Workshop on Computer-aided Language Teaching, Taipei.

Chang, B. (2002). Extraction of Translation Equivalent Pairs from Chinese-English Parallel Corpus. *Terminology Standardization and Information Technology, 2*, 24–29.

Chang, B. (2003). Translation Equivalent Pairs Extraction Based on Statistical Measures. *Chinese Journal of Computers, 26*(5), 616–621.

Chang, B., Zhan, W., & Zhang, H. (2003). Bilingual Corpus Construction and Its Management for Chinese-English Machine Translation. *Terminology Standardization and Information Technology, 1*, 28–31.

Chen, H. (1928). *Yutiwen Yingyong Zihui* [Applied Lexis of Vernacular Chinese]. Beijing Commercial Press.

Chen, W. (2003, July 21–25). *Investigating Explicitation of Conjunctions in Translated Chinese: A Corpus-Based Study.* Paper Presented at the Corpus-Based Translation Studies Conference: Research and Applications, Pretoria, South Africa.

Chen, W. (2006). *Explicitation Through the Use of Connectives in Translated Chinese: A Corpus-Based Study* (Doctoral dissertation). University of Manchester, Manchester.

Chen, J. (2014). Guoneiwai Yuliaoku Kouyi Yanjiu Jinzhan (1998–2012): Yixiang Jiyu Xiangguan Wenxian De Jiliang Yanjiu [An Overview of Corpus-Based Interpreting Studies in China and Abroad (1998–2012): A Quantitative Analysis Based on Literature Review]. *Chinese Translators Journal, 1,* 36–42.

Dai, G., & Xiao, Z. (2010). Jiyu Zijian Yinghan Fanyi Yuliaoku De Fanyi Mingxihua Yanjiu [A Corpus-Based Study of Explicitation in a DIY English-Chinese Translation Corpus]. *Chinese Translators Journal, 1,* 76–80.

Deng, F. (2005). Mianxiang Jiaoxue De Yinghan Shuangyu Pingxing Yuliaoku De Chuangjian Ji Qi Yingyong [The Building and Application of Teaching-Based Chinese-English Parallel Corpus]. *Journal of Huizhou University, 25*(4), 73–76.

Dong, M., & Feng, D. (2015). Yinghan Keji Fanyi Luoji Guanxi Xianhua Celue De Yuliaoku Yanjiu [Explicitation of Logical Links in English-Chinese Technical Translation]. *Foreign Language Education, 36*(2), 93–96.

Frankenberg-Garcia, A. (2002). *Using a Parallel Corpus to Analyse English and Portuguese Translations.* Paper Presented at the Conference of Translation (Studies): A Crossroads of Disciplines, Lisbon.

Gao, Z.-M. (1997). *Automatic Extraction of Translation Equivalents from a Parallel Chinese–English Corpus* (Unpublished PhD thesis). University of Manchester Institute of Science and Technology (UMIST), Manchester.

Guo, H. (2000). *Analysis of University Entrance Examinations, 2000.* Retrieved 28 October 2005, from http://english.lungteng.com.tw/Highschool/information/i6/english/06/89exam.htm.

Harris, Z. (1951). *Methods in Structural Linguistics.* Chicago: University of Chicago Press.

He, X. (2003). Explicitation in English-Chinese Translation. *Journal of PLA University of Foreign Languages, 26*(4), 63–66.

Hu, K., & Mao, P. (2012). Guowai Yuliaoku Fanyi Xue Yanjiu Shuping [An Overview of Corpus-Based Translation Studies Outside China]. *Contemporary Linguistics, 14*(4), 380–395.

Hu, K., Wu, Y., & Qing, T. (2007). Yuliaoku Yu Yixue Yanjiu: Qushi Yu Wenti [Corpora and Translation Studies: Trends and Issues]. *FLC, 5*, 64–69.

Hu, X. (2007). Jiyu Yuliaoku De Hanyu Fanyi Xiaoshuo Ciyu Tezheng Yanjiu [Lexical Features of Translated Chinese Novels: A Corpus-Based Study]. *Foreign Language Teaching and Research, 39*(3), 214–220.

Hu, X., & Zeng, J. (2011). Jiyu Yuliaoku De Fanyi Gongxing Yanjiu Xin Qushi [New Developments in Corpus-Based Study of Translation Universals]. *Journal of PLA University of Foreign Languages, 34*(1), 56–62.

Huang, C. (1997). Interdisciplinary Integration and Integrated Technology: The Role and Development of Computational Linguistics and Corpus Linguistics. *Newsletter of Academia Sinica Computing Center, 13*(23).

Huang, C., & Li, J. (2002). *Yuliaoku Yuyanxue* [Corpus Linguistics]. Beijing: Commercial Press.

Huang, L. (2008). Yinghan Fanyi Zhong Rencheng Daici Zhuyu De Xianhua: Jiyu Yuliaoku De Kaocha [Explicitation of Subjective Personal Pronouns in English-Chinese Translations: A Corpus-Based Study]. *Foreign Language Teaching and Research, 40*(6), 454–459.

Huang, L., & Wang, K. (2011). Yuliaoku Fanyi Xue: Keti Yu Jinzhan [Corpus-Based Translation Studies: Issues and Development]. *Foreign Language Teaching and Research, 43*(6), 911–923.

Huang, L., & Zhu, Z. (2012). Yuliaoku Fanyi Xue: Yanjiu Duixiang Yu Yanjiu Fangfa [Corpus-Based Translation Studies: Objects of Study and Research Methodology]. *FLC, 9*(6), 28–36.

Jiang, T. (2005). Lun Falyu Yuyan Pingxing Yuliaoku De Goujian [On Construction of Forensic Parallel Corpus]. *Journal of Chongqing University (Social Science Edition), 11*(4), 94–97.

Ke, F. (2002). Yuliaoku: Fanyi Yanjiu Xin Tujing [Corpora: A New Approach in Translation Studies]. *Foreign Languages and Their Teaching, 162*, 35–39.

Ke, F. (2005). Implicitation and Explicitation in Translation. *Foreign Language Teaching and Research, 37*(4), 303–307.

Kenny, D. (2000). Translators at Play: Exploitations of Collocational Norms in German-English Translation. In B. Dodd (Ed.), *Working with German Corpora* (pp. 143–160). Birmingham: University of Birmingham Press.

Kenny, D. (2001). *Lexis and Creativity in Translation: A Corpus-Based Study*. Manchester: St. Jerome.

Laviosa-Braithwaite, S. (1996). *The English Comparable Corpus (ECC): A Resource and a Methodology for the Empirical Study of Translation* (Unpublished PhD thesis). UMIST, Manchester.

Laviosa, S. (1997). How Comparable Can 'Comparable Corpora' Be? *Target, 9*(2), 289–319.

Laviosa, S. (1998). Core Patterns of Lexical Use in a Comparable Corpus of English Narrative Prose. *Meta, 43*(4), 557–570.

Laviosa, S. (2002). *Corpus-Based Translation Studies: Theory, Findings, Applications*. Amsterdam and New York: Rodopi.

Leech, G. (1991). The State of the Art in Corpus Linguistics. In K. Aijmer & B. Altenberg (Eds.), *English Corpus Linguistics: Studies in Honour of Jan Svartvik* (pp. 8–29). New York: Longman.

Li, J., & Li, D. (2010). Jiyu Yuliaoku De Kouyi Yanjiu: Huigu Yu Zhanwang [Corpus-Based Interpreting Studies: Review and Prospect]. *Foreign Languages in China, 7*(5), 100–111.

Li, Y. (2014). Jiaoti Chuanyi Zhong Yuzhi Yukuai De Yuyong Shiwu Yanjiu [A Study on Pragmatic Failure of Prefabricated Chunks in Consecutive Interpreting]. *Journal of Guangdong University of Foreign Studies, 5*, 15–19.

Liao, Q. (2000). Yuliaoku Yu Fanyi Yanjiu [Corpora and Translation Studies]. *Foreign Language Teaching and Research, 32*(5), 380–384.

Liou, H., Chang, J. S., Yeh, Y., Liaw, M., Lin, C., Chen, H., et al. (2003). *National Science and Technology Program for E-Learning: CANDLE—Corpora and NLP for Digital Learning of English* (Unpublished manuscript). Taipei.

Liu, M. (2003). *From Empiricism to Constructivism: Researching and Teaching Interpretation.* Paper Presented at the Seventh Conference on the Teaching of Translation and Interpretation, Taipei.

Liu, Y. (2005). Fanyi Guocheng Zhong De Waixianhua Xianxiang Fenxi [An Analysis of Explicitation in Translation]. *Journal of Daxian Teachers College (Social Science Edition), 15*(1), 64–66.

Liu, Z., & Liu, D. (2011). Jiyu Yuliaoku De Fanyi Jiaoxue Yu Xuexizhe Yiben Pingxi Chutan [A Corpus-Based Approach to Teaching Translation and Evaluating Learners' Translations: A Pilot Study]. *FLC, 8*(5), 48–56.

Long, S. (2012). Yuliaoku Fanyi Xue: Wenti Yu Zhanwang [Corpus-Based Translation Studies: Issues and Vision]. *Jiangxi Journal of Social Science, 2012*(12), 244–248.

Luo, X., Dong, N., & Li, T. (2005). Corpora and translation Studies: Reviewing Maeve Olohan's. *Introducing Corpora in Translation Studies Foreign Languages and Their Teaching, 12*, 52–56.

Mao, R. (2003). *Ying Yi Han Jiqiao Xin Bian* [Exploration into New Techniques of English-Chinese Translation]. Beijing: Foreign Languages Press.

Mauranen, A. (2000). Strange Strings in Translated Language: A Study on Corpora. In M. Olohan (Ed.), *Intercultural Faultlines: Research Models in Translation Studies I: Textual and Cognitive Aspects* (pp. 119–141). Manchester: St. Jerome.

Mauranen, A., & Kujamäki, P. (2004). Introduction to *Translation Universals: Do They Exist?* In A. Mauranen & P. Kujamäki (Eds.), *Translation Universals: Do They Exist?* (pp. 1–11). Amsterdam and Philadelphia: John Benjamins.

McEnery, T., & Wilson, A. (2001). *Corpus Linguistics* (2nd ed.). Edinburgh: Edinburgh University Press.

Munday, J. (1998). A Computer-Assisted Approach to the Analysis of Translation Shifts. *Meta, 43*(4), 142–156.

Mutesayire, M. (2005). *Investigating Lexical Explicitation in Translated English: A Corpus-Based Study* (Unpublished PhD thesis). University of Manchester, Manchester.

Olohan, M. (2004). *Introducing Corpora in Translation Studies.* London and New York: Routledge.

Olohan, M., & Baker, M. (2000). Reporting *That* in Translated English: Evidence for Subliminal Processes of Explicitation? *Across Languages and Cultures, 1*(2), 141–158.

Piao, S. S. (2002). Word Alignment in English-Chinese Parallel Corpora. *Literary and Linguistic Computing, 17*(2), 207–230.

Qin, H., & Wang, K. (2004). Jiyu Yuliaoku De Fanyi Yuyan Fenxi: Yi 'so… that' De Hanyu Duiying Jiegou Weili [Parallel Corpora-Based Analysis of Translationese: The English 'So…That' Structure and Its Chinese Equivalents in Focus]. *Modern Foreign Languages, 27*(1), 40–48.

Ren, X. (2014). Fanyi Hanyu Zhong Zhishi Daici De Xianhua: Jiyu Yuliaoku De Yanjiu [A Corpus-Based Study of Explicitation of Demonstrative Pronouns in Translational Chinese]. *Journal of Changshu Institute of Technology, 5,* 91–97.

Renouf, A. (1987). Corpus Development. In J. M. Sinclair (Ed.), *Looking Up: An Account of the COBUILD Project in Lexical Computing* (pp. 1–40). London and Glasgow: Collins.

Shih, C., & Shen, C. (2004). *A Corpus-Based Investigation into Student Technical Translation.* Paper Presented at the Ninth Conference on the Teaching of Interpretation and Translation, Tainan, Taiwan.

Shlesinger, M. (1998). Corpus-Based Interpreting Studies as an Offshoot of Corpus-Based Translation Studies. *Meta, 43*(4), 486–493.

Song, Q., Kuang, H., and Wu. (2013). Guonei Yuliaoku Fanyi Xue Ershi Nian Shuping [Twenty Years of Corpus-Based Translation Studies in China (1993–2012): An Overview]. *Shanghai Journal of Translators, 2,* 25–29.

Straniero, S., Falbo, F., & Fablo, C. (Eds.). (2012). *Breaking Ground in Corpus-Based Interpreting Studies*. Bern: Peter Lang.

Tan, X. (2015). Yingshi Zimu Fanyi Zhong Jiazhu De Yuliaoku Fuzhu Yanjiu [A Corpus-Assisted Analysis of Annotation Method in Subtitle Translation]. *Journal of Luoyang Institute of Science and Technology, 30*(1), 15–18.

Teich, E. (2003). *Cross-Linguistic Variation in System and Text: A Methodology for the Investigation of Translations and Comparable Texts*. Berlin: Mouton de Gruyter.

Tirkkonen-Condit, S. (2002). Translationese—A Myth or an Empirical Fact? A Study into the Linguistic Identifiability of Translated Language. *Target, 14*(2), 207–220.

Tirkkonen-Condit, S. (2004). Unique Items: Over or Under-Represented in Translated Language? In A. Mauranen & P. Kujamäki (Eds.), *Translation Universals: Do they Exist?* John Benjamins: Amsterdam and Philadelphia.

Wang, K. (2003). Yinghan/Hanying Yuju Duiying De Yuliaoku Kaocha [Sentence Parallelism in English–Chinese/Chinese–English: A Corpus-Based Investigation]. *Foreign Language Teaching and Research, 35*(6), 410–416.

Wang, K. (2004a). Shuangyu Pingxing Yuliaoku Zai Fanyi Jiaoxue Shang De Yongtu [The Use of Parallel Corpora in Translator Training]. *ETFLT, 100,* 27–32.

Wang, K. (2004b). Xinxing Shuangyu Duiying Yuliaoku De Sheji Yu Goujian [Design and Construction of a New Bi-lingual Corpus]. *Chinese Translators Journal, 25*(6), 73–75.

Wang, K., & Hu, X. (2008). Jiyu Yuliaoku De Fanyi Hanyu Cihui Tezheng Yanjiu [A Corpus-Based Study of Lexical Features in Translated Chinese]. *Chinese Translators Journal, 6,* 16–21.

Wang, K., Qin, H., & Wang, H. (2007). Shuangyu Duiying Yuliaoku Fanyi Jiaoxue Pingtai De Yingyong Chutan [Using Bi-directional Parallel Corpora as a Platform of Translation Teaching: A Pilot Study]. *CAFLE, 118,* 3–8.

Wang, L. (2001). 'yi…jiu…' De Zhongzhong Yingyi [Various Ways of Chinese–English Translation of a Chinese Phrase 'yi…jiu…']. *Chinese Science & Technology Translators Journal, 14*(2), 60–61.

Wei, S., & Li, S. (2013). Yuliaoku Fanyi Xue Fazhan Xianzhuang Ji Zhuanxiang [Corpus-Based Translation Studies: Current Status and Turns]. *Journal of Changchun University, 23*(7), 856–861.

Wu, G. (2000). 'That' Yongfa Chutan [Exploring Various Usage of 'That']. *Journal of Zhejiang Normal University, 25*(3), 93–97.

Xiao, W. (2005). Zijian Yuliaoku Yu Fanyi Piping [DIY Corpora and Translation Criticism]. *Foreign Languages Research, 92,* 60–65.

Xiao, Z. (2012). *Yinghan Fanyi Zhong Hanyu Yiwen Yuliaoku Yanjiu* [A Corpus-Based Study of English-Chinese Translations]. Shanghai: Shanghai Jiao Tong University Press.

Xiao, Z., & Dai, G. (2010). Xunzhao 'Di San Yuma': Jiyu Hanyu Yiwen Yuliaoku De Fanyi Gongxing Yanjiu [In Search of the 'Third Code': A Corpus-Based Study of Universals in Translated Chinese]. *Foreign Language Teaching and Research, 42*(1), 52–58.

Xie, J. (2004a). 'yi…jiu' De Yingyi: Jian Tan Yinghan Pingxing Yuliaoku Fuzhu Han Yi Ying Diaocha [Various English Translations of the Chinese Phrase 'yi…jiu': From the Perspective of Individual English and Chinese Parallel Corpus]. *Chinese Science & Technology Translators Journal, 17*(2), 27–29.

Xie, J. (2004b). Xiaoxing Yinghan Pingxing Yuliaoku De Jianli Yu Yingyong [Construction and Application of a Small English and Chinese Parallel Corpus]. *Journal of PLA University of Foreign Languages, 27*(3), 45–48.

Xu, J., & Zi, Z. (2014). Jiyu Yuliaoku De Yingyu Caijing Xinwen Hanyi Ben De Cihui Tezheng Yanjiu [A Corpus-Based Study on the Lexical Features of Chinese Translation of English Business News]. *FLC, 11*(5), 66–74.

Yang, X. (2007). Jiyu Yuliaoku Fanyi Yanjiu He Yizhe Jiaoyu [A Corpus-Based Approach to Translation Studies and Translator Education]. *Foreign Languages and Their Teaching, 223,* 51–55.

Zanettin, F., Bernardini, S., & Stewart, D. (Eds.). (2003). *Corpora in Translator Education*. Manchester: St. Jerome.

Zhang, L., & Hu, D. (2011). Guonei Jiyu Yuliaoku De Fanyi Yanjiu De Fazhan [An Overview of Corpus-Based Translation Studies in China]. *Journal of Jiaxing University, 23*(2), 95–99.

Zhen, F., & Zhang, X. (2004). Yuliaoku Yuyanxue Fazhan Qushi Zhanwang. *Foreign Language World, 102,* 74–77.

Zhu, Y., & Hu, K. (2014). 'Bei' Zi Ju De Yuyi Quxiang Yu Yuyiyun– Jiyu Fanyi Yu Yuanchuang Xinwen Yuliaoku De Duibi Yanjiu [Semantic Preferences and Semantic Prosody of Bei Passives: A Corpus-Based Contrastive Study]. *Journal of Foreign Languages, 37*(1), 53–64.

The Role of Translation Played in the Evolution of Mandarin: A Corpus-based Account

Hongwu Qin, Lei Kong and Ranran Chu

1 Introduction

Language changes over time, evolving in many ways for a variety of reasons. Of the factors contributing to language change, translation—a form of indirect language contact—has long been regarded as a minor factor. However, it is also documented that translational language may play a critical role in the evolution of a language. For example, Martin Luther's translation of the Bible into German (completed in 1534) and his creative use of the German vernacular had a long-lasting effect on the development of the German language (Kittle and Poltermann 2009: 414). In a similar way, in the early decades of the twentieth century, translational Mandarin played an important role in the reformation of Mandarin *baihua* (白话), as observed in Wang (1947: 334–373) and He (2008), who listed a fairly detailed

H. Qin (✉) · L. Kong · R. Chu
Qufu Normal University, Qufu, China

K. Hu and K. H. Kim (eds.), *Corpus-based Translation and Interpreting Studies in Chinese Contexts*, Palgrave Studies in Translating and Interpreting,
https://doi.org/10.1007/978-3-030-21440-1_2

enumeration of the linguistic features acquired under the influence of translational Mandarin and ranked syntactic complexity as one of the major changes (Wang 1947: 346). However, little is said about the factors contributing to this complexity. To offer an adequate account of these factors, this study examines the way in which Mandarin underwent a sudden increase in its syntactic complexity (reflected in the use of longer sentences). Our focus is on a construction's load capacity (CLC), which can best explain how the complexity of a Mandarin sentence is built up.

A 'construction', as used in Goldberg (2002: 4), refers to the basic unit of a language, a clause, or an independent phrasal pattern, such as V-NP-ADJ (e.g. *hammer the metal flat*), that pairs form with meaning. For Mandarin, a construction can be a phrasal pattern as shown in Examples (1)–(3).

Example (1)

在 你 熟悉 的 王先生 家里 [Preposition…NP-Localizer]
[Gloss] ZAI you familiar DE$_{_relativizer}$ Mr. Wang home *loc*[1]
in the home of Mr. Wang with whom you are familiar.

Example (2)

一-位 六十 多 岁 的 老 工人 [Number-Classifier…NP]
[Gloss] Num-CL sixty more year DE$_{_relativizer}$ old worker
an old worker who is over sixty.

Example (3)

那-幢 刚 建好 的 红色 的 大楼 [Demonstrative-Classifier…NP]
[Gloss] Dem-CL just build well DE$_{_relativizer}$ red DE building
the red building that was just built up.

[1]The term *loc* stands for localizer in Mandarin; Num stands for number; CL stands for classifier, or a measure word. For example, 一-头 is composed by 一 (Num, 'one') and 头 (CL, 'head').

In this study, we look into the complexity[2] (see Sect. 2.2 for more information on this term) of the elements contained in these constructions. We will observe the complexity in grammatical features, not just in terms of the number of words (Wang and Qin 2014).

2 Load Capacity and Information Processing

Language is linear in nature. '[W]ords as used in discourse, strung together one after another, enter into relations based on the linear character of languages' (de Saussure 1983: 121). This linearity suggests words are arranged in terms of syntagmatic relations, which means that the similarity and the difference between languages can be found in the ordering of elements. As is shown in Example (3), in Mandarin, modifiers (*just build well DE* $_{\_relativizer}$ and *red DE building*) are typically placed before the modified (*building*). Mandarin does not allow right-branching modifiers, thus it is structurally close-ended. For English, however, we can put a postmodifier after the modified (as in the English version '*that was just built up*'). Relative pronouns, participle phrases, or prepositional phrases in English make it possible to place modifiers after the modified (as indicated in the English versions in Examples (1)–(3)); hence, it is structurally open-ended.

With Mandarin being structurally close-ended, how does this increase its syntactic complexity? The answer to the question can only be found in the analysis of its intra-structural properties.

2.1 The LC of a Construction

As noted, Mandarin constructions are 'close-ended' (Wang and Qin 2014), and the elements at the two ends are major elements in processing. If there is too long a distance (usually defined by the number of

[2]According to Douglas and Miller (2016), factors with significant correlations with complexity across writing and reading samples are lexile, mean length sentence (MLS), mean length clause (MLC), and complex nominals per T-unit (CN/T). In our research, the length of the modifiers, the number of modifiers, and the use of pre-positioned clausal modifiers all contribute to syntactic complexity.

words or modifiers a construction accommodates) between them (the beginning and the ending words in Examples (1)–(3)), it will overburden the processor's working memory, and make it difficult to process the main elements. Perhaps it is one of the major reasons that Mandarin often uses short and separate clauses or segments[3] to express meaning, even when the meaning is complex. This is evidenced by Wang and Qin (2014), who argue that a Mandarin construction does not welcome the insertion of long and complex modifiers, and that a Mandarin sentence would contain more segments than its English equivalent does.

Among those close-ended constructions in Mandarin, the active[4] ones are Preposition + Locative (P-L), Numeral Classifier + NP (NC-NP) and Demonstrative Classifier + NP (DC-NP). P-L is functionally similar to English prepositional phrases (location of time and place), and NC-NP and DC-NP are similar to an English NP. But, in contrast with English, the three constructions do not allow for post-nominal modifiers. In what follows, we mainly observe P-L and DC-NP constructions in a diachronic perspective.[5]

2.2 CLC and Cognitive Processing

The length of a clause usually associates with structural complexity. The longer the sentence (clause) is, the more likely that multiple discrete ideas, called 'propositions', are embedded in it (Arya et al. 2011). So, generally, if length is measured by the number of words in a syntactic unit, then the sum of words is in proportion to syntactic complexity (Szmrecsányi 2004). However, this is not always the case. Clauses of the same length do not necessarily mean that they are of the same syntactic

[3]As is found in Ji (2010: 39–40), in translating multilayered Castilian sentences into Mandarin (the same is true for translation from English to Mandarin), the long sentences in the source text tend to get broken down into a number of relatively shorter clauses, and these elements are then rearranged or inserted in specific positions of a sentential sequence that is familiar to the Mandarin readership.

[4]By active, we mean they are major sentence constituents used to locate events in time and place (P-L), or to act as subjects or objects (NC-NP or DC-NP).

[5]We choose not to talk about NC-NP construction in the present study, for the construction is also contained in the P-L construction, or partially overlaps with the DC-NP construction.

complexity. Taking this into consideration, we only use the length of a construction as a clue in data retrieval; what we delve into, however, is the internal structure of constructions.

A syntactic structure is both formal and psychological, for a speaker usually constructs and produces grammatically well-formed linguistic material in line with their own intention and preference. This is why Szmrecsányi (2004) puts forward the Index of Syntactic Complexity (ISC) to link language uses with cognitive processing. Based on Beaman (1984: 45) and Givón (1991), he classifies clauses (such as *SUB*, *that*) and a variety of embedded elements (such as *WH*, *which*) as ISC. Although ISC may be applicable to English, it is not to Mandarin, since the latter lacks connective devices such as relative clauses to place a post-nominal modifier. Mandarin only has pre-positioning devices such as attributives marked by auxiliary *DE*, as in Example (4), where DE (a relativizer) has the dual function that English *that (SUB)* and *WH* have, though the former only allows for pre-nominal use.

Example 4

a. 我来到这个 曾经 听 得 那么多 的 地方
b. I come to this-CL once hear of de so much DE$_{_relativizer}$ place
c. I arrived at the place where I had heard of so much.

Then, what is the relationship between syntactic complexity and readability? As Givón (2009: 12) puts it, syntactic complexity in linguistics correlates with cognitive complexity. Roughly, the possible correlations may be listed as follows: (i) Coding: more complex mentally represented events are coded by more complex linguistic, specifically syntactic, structures; (ii) Processing-I: more complex mentally represented events require more complex mental processing operations; and (iii) Processing-II: more complex syntactic structures require more complex mental processing operations.

The correlations suggest that syntactic complexity is highly relevant to processing costs. If that is true, we can evaluate the ease of processing by observing the syntactic complexity. But what accounts for such complexity? The answer to the question can partly be found in the patterns of encoding of conceptual elements by particular types of surface forms.

Languages may use different devices to encode an event or semantic relations, as is illustrated by the translation pair in Example (5), with the Mandarin source text (ST) and its English target text (TT).

Example (5)

a. 汽车夫轻声地对坐 在 他 旁边 的 穿 一身 黑 拷绸 衣裤 的 彪形 大汉说:
[Gloss] Car man light voice to sit beside him DE $_{\_relativizer}$ wear whole body black silk clothes DE $_{\_relativizer}$ husky fellow say:
b. The driver said in a low voice to the hulking fellow sitting beside him in black silk.

The Mandarin ST and English TT, shown respectively in Examples (5a) and (5b), feature different uses of syntactic devices to encode the modifier-modified relations. In Mandarin ST, the clausal modifier 穿 一身 黑 拷绸 衣裤 的 (wear whole-body black silk clothes DE) functions as an attributive, whereas it is expressed in a prepositional phrase *in black silk* in the English TT. Also, another clausal modifier 坐 在 他 旁边 的 (sit beside him DE) in Example (5a) is rendered into a present participle phrase *sitting beside him* in Example (5b). Examples (5a) and (5b) show that English, which is both a left-branching and right-branching language, has two options for placing modifiers: either pre-nominal or post-nominal. In contrast, a modified construction in Mandarin only takes pre-nominal modifiers. Moreover, Example (5) suggests that English, with its flexibility in using pre-nominal or post-nominal modifiers, has devices to realize structural symmetry. Mandarin, however, with all the modifiers being pre-nominal, is prone to structural overload or complexity if a close-ended construction accommodates too many modifiers.

If the amount of information and syntactic complexity are in correlation with processing effort, Example (5a) should require more processing effort than Example (5b), in that the latter is syntactically symmetrical, with the modifiers being put around the modified; hence, a processing that needs less working memory. In contrast, the processing of Example (5a) needs more working memory, as the reader has to process all the complex modifiers before processing what is being modified.

This may help to explain why Mandarin rarely takes complex modifiers. Instead, Mandarin often uses separate clauses to present the modification relations.[6] However, the use of multiple and complex modifiers in Example (5a) does challenge our conception of normal modifier use in Mandarin, and there must be some reasons underlying this use.

As a language with close-ended constructions, Mandarin is sensitive to CLC (Qin 2010; Wang and Qin 2009, 2014), and LC can serve as a good index for difficulty in processing Chinese. However, most of the comparative studies carried out on LC have so far failed to address the issue from a diachronic perspective.

The present study adopts a corpus-based approach to a diachronic comparison between original Mandarin and translated Mandarin, analysing the elements in the close-ended constructions and inquiring into various factors involved in LC change. In what follows, we will present the research questions and the research method.

3 Research Questions and Methodology

3.1 Research Questions

As discussed in Sect. 2, linguistic complexity can be measured by the number of words, the number of modifiers, and the length of modifiers in a clause. For Mandarin, the complexity is also measured by the number of words and the complexity of pre-nominal modifiers used in a construction. As has been mentioned, length and syntactic complexity are not entirely the same. Length is measured by the number of words, while complexity is evaluated by referring to the syntactic intricacy of the elements in a construction. Grammatically, complexity is a rather

[6]A typical Mandarin encoding of the relations in Example (5a) could be as follows:

彪形 大汉 坐 在 他 旁边,穿 一身 黑 拷绸 衣裤。 汽车夫 轻声地 对 他 说:

[Gloss] husky fellow sit beside him, wear whole body black silk clothes. Car man says in a low voice to him.

In this Mandarin encoding, more clauses are used, which is a typical way of encoding such relation.

relative concept. Other things being equal, a clause is more complex than a phrase or a word, and a clausal modifier is more complex than a one-word modifier. Taking that into consideration, a long string of words or many modifiers may not lead to complexity or reduced readability. For instance, in the examples below, there are more than four modifiers in the close-ended constructions (the underlined parts).

Example (6)

他是中国第一个能跑、 能跳、能投、能盖帽 以及 能参与快攻 的 全能中锋 (LCMC)

[Gloss] he is China's first can run, can jump, can shoot, can block shots and can participate in fast attack DE $_{\text{relativizer}}$ do-it-all center

He is the first do-it-all center in China, who is adept in running, jumping, shooting, shots blocking and fast attacking.

Example (7)

只要得个相貌端正、性情贤慧、持得家 吃得苦 的 孩子, (COB1911)

[Gloss] only need a looking fair, temperament kind, manage family eat bitterness DE $_{\text{relativizer}}$ child

We only need a boy who is good-looking, kind-hearted, thrifty and hardworking.

In Mandarin, these clauses, with multiple modifiers, are not low in readability in that the parallel structures therein make it easy for readers to process them. Considering that, we cannot stop at a simple length calculation for the analysis of LC. We need to turn to clausal modifiers or modifiers with embedded elements for an adequate analysis of the load capacity. Thus, we use CLC to refer to complexity of the elements in Mandarin close-ended construction. In what follows, how CLC in Mandarin evolved in the twentieth century will be discussed.

Now that we have ascertained that a Mandarin construction is close-ended, and it is sensitive to the load capacity of a construction, we can observe the role played by translation in the evolution of Mandarin from a CLC perspective. And, considering that the adequate account of the load capacity theoretically lies in syntactic complexity (the use of modifiers or embedded elements), our account of CLC will mainly revolve around the use of syntactically complex elements.

3.2 Methodology and Data Collection

To observe how Mandarin changed in the early decades of the twentieth century, we use a diachronic corpus (the original Mandarin corpus in Table 1) as empirical data. To depict the probable relations between translational Mandarin and original Mandarin, we use comparable corpora (the original Mandarin corpus and translational Mandarin corpus in Table 1).

As Table 1 shows, the diachronic comparable corpus consists of two separate subcorpora: the diachronic original Mandarin corpus (monolingual) and the translational Mandarin corpus (bilingual, parallel). The diachronic original Mandarin corpus is made up of several subcorpora, among which is LCMC, a balanced corpus of Mandarin (2003), and the other two newly built original Mandarin corpora. The Translational Mandarin corpus, however, consists of GCEPC (2004) and the E-C translation corpus (1919–1930s).

To obtain close-ended Mandarin constructions, first, we have to unravel their position in a sentence. We find that Mandarin close-ended constructions are usually found in the middle of a sentence, as in Example (8), where the underlined parts form a close-ended 'ZAI...*loc*' construction.

Example (8)

他们在 明亮 的 教室 里 学习。
[Gloss]They ZAI bright DE classroom *loc* learn.
They are working in a bright classroom.

As the preposition 'ZAI' and the localizer '*loc*' mark the two ends of a construction, they are used to begin and end the regular expression for

Table 1 Diachronic comparable corpus of Mandarin

	Parallel corpus	Subcorpus	Capacity (words)	Components
Comparable diachronic corpora	Original Mandarin corpus	Original Mandarin before 1911 (COB1911)[a]	1,229,128	Traditional *baihua*: Literature: 1,136,056 (92%); non-literature (press) 93,112 (8%). Most of them are *baihua* novels, small amount of *baihua* press, no scientific works
		Original Mandarin (1919[b]–1930s)	1,236,273	New *baihua*: Literature: 1,029,263 (83%); non-literature: 207,010 (17%). Mostly *baihua* literary writings, greater percentage of non-literature
		LCMC (1991–)[c]	83,4007	Contemporary Mandarin: balanced corpus
	Translational Mandarin corpus	E-C Translation corpus (1919–1930s)	2,713,469	Translation in New *baihua*: Literature: 1,193,695 (43%); non-literature: 1,519,774 (56%)
		GCEPC(1980–)	2,123,097	Translation in contemporary Mandarin: Literature: 1,006,694 (47%); non-literature: 1,116,403 (53%). Relatively balanced
	Total	Comparable corpus	8,051,381	

[a]COB1911 refers to Original Mandarin before 1911. In the history of China, the 1911 revolution marks China's transition from a feudal society to a capitalist society, and also suggests that Mandarin before 1911 was rarely influenced by the Western language

[b]The year 1919 marks a special cultural movement that aimed at creating new cultural and literary norms. The movement also advocated that changes in Mandarin be made by imitating certain features of European languages, with English being the first choice for that purpose

[c]LCMC refers to Lancaster Corpus of Mandarin; GCEPC refers to the General Corpus of Chinese–English Parallel Corpus (this study only uses the corpus after 1980)

data retrieval. In addition, part of speech (POS) tags are used to filter out irrelevant data. Thus, we use Perl to write the program for extracting data from the corpora. Below is the relevant part of the program, where '\S+' stands for any group of letters (e.g. a word), and 'm', 'q', 'r', 'f', and 'nd' stand for the part of speech, such as number, classifier,

Norms and Norm-Taking in Interpreting for Chinese Government Press Conferences: A Case Study of Hedges

Feng Pan

1 Introduction

As a special type of interaction, interpreting, like any other communicative activity, is subject to the powerful constraints of norms. Norms function to regulate behaviour and to reduce the variation in language use, contributing to the establishment of social stability and solidarity. In diplomatic settings, where every word may have a serious bearing, interpreters are usually required to translate the speaker's remarks closely and faithfully. It is generally expected that, constrained by such powerful norms, interpreters' subjectivity is very limited and they are largely 'invisible' (see Harris 1990) in diplomatic settings. In addition, as interpreting is a cognitively demanding task, the professional training received by interpreters usually guides them to give priority to the propositional meanings in cross-linguistic transfer (Gile 2009; Seleskovitch 1977). Hedges, as a rhetorical means, belong to the metadiscourse

F. Pan (✉)
Huazhong University of Science and Technology, Wuhan, China
e-mail: fengpan@hust.edu.cn

K. Hu and K. H. Kim (eds.), *Corpus-based Translation and Interpreting Studies in Chinese Contexts*, Palgrave Studies in Translating and Interpreting,
https://doi.org/10.1007/978-3-030-21440-1_4

and are typically not part of the propositional meaning in discourse. Therefore, it can be expected that, with the 'faithfulness' and 'propositional meaning first' norms at work, hedges are more likely to be omitted when interpreters are confronted with huge cognitive load. However, many previous studies have revealed the opposite trend, where interpreters frequently manipulate (e.g. add or substitute) hedges of various kinds for different purposes (e.g. Sun 2014; Wang 2013). This shows that interpreters are also subject to other norms beyond those we mentioned above, which function together to impact on interpreters' choices.

Against the above backdrop, this study investigates interpreters' use of hedges in Chinese government press conference interpreting using a corpus (see Sect. 3). The aim of this study is to identify the various norms at work in interpreting and the effect that their interplay has on interpreters' choices. For contrastive analysis, this study also selects the translations of Chinese government Work Reports as a reference, in order to identify any differences of norms between interpreting and translation.

2 Research Background

The term 'norms', which has its origin in sociology, refers to a social group's expectation or notion about what is correct or appropriate. Gideon Toury (1978) was the first to introduce the term into translation studies and use it as a category to describe translational phenomena. Norms are defined by Toury as 'the translation of general values or ideas shared by a community—as to what is right and wrong, adequate and inadequate—into performance instructions appropriate for and applicable to particular situations' (Toury 1995: 54–55). He views translation as an activity situated in particular social historical contexts, constrained by the norms prevailing in that society.

Shlesinger (1989: 111) was the pioneer who explored the possibility of extending the notion of translational norms into interpreting studies. Specifically, she examined the factors 'which encumber both the formation and extrapolation of norms' (Shlesinger 1989: 111), such as the difficulty of assembling a representative corpus. Later, scholars such as Harris (1990) and Gile (1999: 99–105) also discussed the possibility and necessity of researching norms in interpreting. In particular, Gile argued that interpreters' strategies are not totally cognitively determined, but are usually norm-based; that is, interpreters are accustomed to making choices complying with certain norms. Following their discussions, more attention has been invested in norms in interpreting.

In the Chinese context, a few empirical studies have been carried out to probe into norms in interpreting. Hu and Tao (2012), based on a transcribed corpus, explored operational norms at the syntactic level in Chinese–English conference interpreting. This analysis shows that the impact of explicitation and complication is more noticeable than implicitation and simplification at the syntactic level. This work argued that the different degrees of formalization between Chinese and English explain these findings. Wang (2012) investigates the relational norms between target texts (TT) and source texts (ST) from the interpreted press conferences of Chinese premiers with 'shifts' as the analytical tool. The research ultimately identified four typical norms of ST–TT relations: adequacy, explicitation in logic relations, specificity in information content, and explicitness in meaning. These studies have contributed to a more solid understanding of norms in Chinese interpreting, both at theoretical and empirical levels.

However, few studies have inquired into the norms governing interpreters' choices in metadiscourse, though they are manipulated for a variety of purposes on a regular basis in interpreting. This study therefore attempts to fill the gap in this regard with hedges as a case in point.

3 Research Design: A Functional Model of Hedges, Data and Methodology

Hedges can have a variety of functions in discourse, such as expressing uncertainty or modesty, or limiting a speaker's commitment to a proposition. Scholars, however, have now generally agreed on the 'multi-functionality and heterogeneity' (Namsaraev 1997: 68) of hedges, though no shared definition of hedge has been reached. Along with Holmes' call that any useful description of the distribution of hedges 'clearly requires a prior functional analysis' (1986: 1), the study adapts Hyland's (1996a, b) categorization as a functional model for analysis, as it offers 'a useful amalgamation of earlier approaches to hedging' and succeeds in 'providing a useful taxonomy of the various functions that a given hedge may have' (Varttala 2001: 89–90). Hedges are defined as 'any linguistic means used to indicate either: (i) a lack of complete commitment to the truth of a proposition; or (ii) a desire not to express that commitment categorically' (Hyland 1996a: 251) and, mainly, can be divided into accuracy oriented, writer oriented, and reader oriented functions.

Accuracy oriented hedges involve the speaker's desire to express something with greater precision (Hyland 1996a). This type of hedge is used to express uncertain claims with appropriate caution and aims to avoid the risk of falsification on objective grounds. They usually work within propositions modifying individual words or phrases. Speaker oriented or writer oriented hedges express the speaker's assessment or evaluation of the truth of the propositional content, but do not affect the truth-value of the proposition itself as accuracy oriented hedges do. They are characterized by a lack of the speaker's agency in discourse. Both accuracy oriented and speaker oriented hedges are content motivated, in that they modify the relationship between what the speaker states about the world and what the world actually is. Though content motivated hedges reflect considerations on objective grounds, audience (or reader) oriented hedges involve avoiding the risk of negation or rejection on subjective grounds by granting a role for the hearer. They function to facilitate the interpersonal relationship between interlocutors, indicating the attention the speaker is willing to give to their partner. They serve to mitigate the illocutionary force of a speech act either to show deference, politeness, or humility towards those listening, and reflect the speaker's desire to be understood and accepted by the audience. Audience oriented hedges are marked by clear reference to the speaker, or by addressing the hearers and/or their readership directly, implying that the proposition is only an alternative and personal interpretation, rather than a conclusive one.

In terms of the data, a corpus was built for this study that consists of two separate subcorpora: (i) the parallel corpus of interpreting for

Chinese government press conferences and (ii) the parallel corpus of translations of Chinese government Work Reports for reference purposes. For the interpreting subcorpus, all the materials are authentic and were drawn from the Chinese government press conferences held during the annual National People's Congress and the Chinese People's Political Consultative Conference (commonly known as the 'two sessions') from the year 1990 to 2014. During the press conferences, the premier or foreign minister would answer questions from both Chinese and international journalists, with a consecutive interpreting service provided between Chinese and English after each turn. For data homogeneity, those occasional questions initiated in English and interpreted into Chinese were eliminated from our data to ensure that all the materials were from Chinese to English. All the recorded source discourses and their interpreted counterparts were first transcribed into machine readable texts, following which they were aligned at sentence level using the software ParaConc. The resultant transcribed ST include 253,904 Chinese characters and the TT consist of 201,924 English words. For the translation subcorpus, all the materials were collected from the annual Chinese government Work Reports and their official translations from the year 1992 to 2014, accessible from official websites such as Xinhua.com. This subcorpus comprises 307,524 characters in Chinese and 255,641 words in English. The two subcorpora are, therefore, comparable in terms of topics, genre, time span, and size.

Translational norms are not directly observable but are manifested in norm-governed behaviour—more precisely, the products of such behaviour. Toury (1995: 65) proposed two ways to reconstruct norms, using: (i) textual sources and (ii) extra-textual sources. Textual sources are the translated texts themselves. Extra-textual sources include 'prescriptive "theories" of translation, statements made by translators, editors, publishers, and other persons involved in or connected with the activity, critical appraisals of individual translations, or the activity of a translator or "school" of translators, and so forth' (Toury 1995: 65). Gile (1999: 100) specifically argued that research into norms in interpreting can be done by 'asking interpreters about norms, by reading didactic, descriptive and narrative texts about interpreting'; that is, extra-textual sources. This study combines both textual and extra-textual sources.

Textual sources include both analysis of TTs and analysis of the ST–TT relation. First, this study takes Hyland's (2005) and Holmes' (1988) lists of hedging items as the point of departure from which to identify hedges (see Appendix for a full list of hedges examined in this study), and analyses their functions in the interpreted and translated texts. It is expected that the results of the analysis in this step will be able to discern the norms of interaction in TTs using hedges. Second, this study aims, through analysis of the parallel texts, to identify interpreters' regular strategic choices and the optional shifts between ST and TT. 'Shift', here, refers to the small changes 'that build up cumulatively over a whole text as a result of the choices taken by or imposed on the translator' (Munday 1998: 542). This step is carried out based on the assumption that translational norms manifest themselves in interpreters' regular options. The identification of interpreters' behaviour on a regular basis makes norms observable.

At the same time, the study collects data of metadiscourse on diplomatic interpreting, interviews with interpreters, and statements about language use in linguistics and in the interpreting profession. It tries to identify the various factors influencing interpreters' behaviour by analysing the attitude of the interpreting profession or interpreting institution towards norms. By so doing, the study combines both textual and extra-textual sources to reconstruct the norms governing interpreters' choice of hedges in interpreting.

4 Analysis

In this section, the distributional features of hedges in translated and interpreted texts are presented first, followed by an analysis into the translating and interpreting process identifying occurrences of 'shift'.

4.1 Distributional Features of Hedges in Target Texts

The analysis of the interpreted and translated texts reveals a wide variety of surface forms of hedges that fulfil a primarily accuracy oriented, speaker oriented, or audience oriented function. The underlined words in the following examples illustrate their occurrences in context:

Example (1)

I/Qian: The second set of figures that I'll, I'd like to give you is that, the per capita military spending in China is only about 6 US dollars, whereas for the United States, it's 1100 and for Japan, it's 300.

Example (2)

I/Wen: I wish to conclude by quoting from an ancient Indian scripture, probably written more than 3000 years ago in Sanskrit.

Example (3)

I/Wen: People generally believe that this marks the entering of a more complicated stage in cross-straits relations.

Example (4)

I/Zhu: So, in terms of the number of these loss-making state-owned enterprises, it seems that the loss-making percentage is very high.

Example (5)

I/Zhu: I think some foreign media have overestimated or played up the difficulties of China's state-owned enterprises.

Example (6)

I/Li: According to my knowledge, and my knowledge might not be that comprehensive, in 2005 alone, the administrative authorities for industry and commerce in China had investigated and dealt with more than thirty-nine thousand cases of trade mark infringement.

In Example (1), the exact number for China's military spending per capita is hedged by 'about', which indicates that the stated number approximates to, but may not equate exactly with, the actual number. In Example (2), 'probably' denotes the speaker's reservation towards the truth of the proposition 'written more than 3000 years ago in Sanskrit'. In both instances, the underlined hedges serve a primarily accuracy oriented function. In Examples (3) and (4), the underlined words 'believe' and 'seems' suggest each speaker's desire to keep distance from an unsubstantiated assertion that follows, thus both serve as a mainly speaker oriented function. In Example (5), the use of 'I think' attenuates the criticism or disagreement encoded in the subsequent statement by acknowledging it as only a personal opinion, rather than a definitive one. As a result, the hedge fulfils a primarily audience oriented function to facilitate interpersonal relationships. The same is true of Example (6), where the phase 'in our view' clearly signifies the speaker's responsibility for the subsequent claim, thus leaving room for negotiation to audience.

As noted, detailed manual analysis is carried out for each hedge in context to identify its main function in the interpreted and translated texts. Table 1 summarizes the functional distribution of hedges across the three categories in the two subcorpora.

On the whole, interpreted texts surpass translated texts markedly in terms of the overall raw frequencies and normalized frequencies in the use of hedges. This difference is also reinforced by the fact that the raw frequencies and normalized frequencies of each functional category in interpreted texts are also higher than those in translated texts. In addition, in terms of functional distribution, the two subcorpora display different patterns. In interpreted texts, hedges are most frequently used to facilitate interpersonal relationships; that is, audience oriented (49.7%). They are also frequently used to enhance the precision of statements (i.e. accuracy oriented: 44.4%) but seldom used to limit speaker's commitment to truth propositions (i.e. speaker oriented: 5.9%). This result indicates interpreters' attempts to make the interpreted texts highly interactive and accurate through the choice of hedges. In contrast, as many as 91.7% of hedges are used to increase the accuracy of statements (i.e. accuracy oriented) in translated texts, but are only rarely used to limit the writer's commitment (i.e. speaker oriented: 5.8%), or to engage readers in interaction (i.e. reader oriented: 2.6%). This result indicates translators' efforts to render the translated texts more accurately. The above difference in the use of hedges between interpreted and translated texts reflects the difference between interpreters' and translators' focus in terms of interactional goals. However, this

Table 1 Functional distribution across categories in interpreted and translated texts[a]

	Accuracy oriented		Speaker/writer oriented		Audience/reader oriented		Total (100%)
	Frequency	Percentage	Frequency	Percentage	Frequency	Percentage	
Interpreted texts	627 (31.1)	44.4	83 (4.1)	5.9	701 (34.7)	49.7	1411 (69.9)
Translated texts	395 (15.5)	91.7	25 (1)	5.8	11 (0.4)	2.6	431 (16.9)

[a]In each column, the raw frequency is followed by its normalized frequency per 10,000 words in parentheses

difference may be from the interference of the ST, or from interpreters'/translators' optional choices, which is to be explored in the next section through the analysis of the interpreting/translating process.

4.2 Analysis of the Interpreting and Translating Process

With the aid of ParaConc, this study has identified four types of correspondence relationship between the identified hedges in the TT and their Chinese ST, or, simply, four types of strategy: *direct transfer, indirect transfer, substitution*, and *addition*, which are summarized in Table 2 with detailed descriptions of the features of each type in the examples given.

As can be seen from Table 2, either in *direct transfer* or *indirect transfer*, the identified TT hedges derive from their ST equivalents, meaning

Table 2 Types of correspondence between identified hedges and the source texts

Types	Description	Examples
Direct transfer	An identified hedge transfers the form and function directly from the ST item	ST: 也许就不需要再发这种建设性的国债了 TT: or perhaps there is no need at all to issue any treasury bonds to undertake those construction projects
Indirect transfer	An identified hedge transfers the hedging function of the ST item or structure, but differs in form	ST: 还给出了指标, 说可能是3%到4% TT: China's growth would slide to about 3–4%
Substitution	An identified hedge has a corresponding ST item (mostly intensifiers) with no hedging function	ST: 基本养老的参与人数也超过8亿人 TT: now the basic old-age insurance schemes cover about 800 million people
Addition	An identified hedge is added by the interpreter with no corresponding ST item	ST: 如您所知,中国最高法院呢已经收回了死刑的核准权 TT: as you may know, the Supreme People's Court of China has taken back the power to approve death penalty

that no extra hedge has been added to the TT by interpreters. However, in cases marked as *substitution* or *addition*, interpreters either substitute an intensifier (or similar item) with a hedge in the TT, or add an additional hedge in the TT without a corresponding item in the ST. Hence, *direct transfer* and *indirect transfer* are marked as 'equivalence' because hedges are transferred from ST items, and *substitution* and *addition* as 'shift' because hedges are brought about by interpreters in the interpreting process. It is notable that these shifts are optional as they are not necessitated by the systemic differences between English and Chinese (alternative choices for equivalence are available) but, rather, are the result of interpreters' individual preferences, or are brought about by various socio-cultural factors imposed on interpreters. They are carried out either consciously or unconsciously by interpreters, and 'give expression to translator's decision-making, and are explicit markers of translational norms' (Wang 2013: 82). The frequencies and distribution of these 'optional shifts' across each functional category provide access to uncovering interpreters' regular behaviour during the interpreting process.

In a similar way, it is found that the above four interpreting strategies can also be used to describe the translating strategies in translated texts. Table 3 summarizes the 'equivalence' and 'shift' cases in terms of hedges in both interpreted and translated texts.

The following patterns can be observed in Table 3. First, with regard to interpreting, the raw and normalized frequencies of 'equivalence' surpass those of 'shift' cases across all functional categories of hedges. 'Shift' cases fall most frequently in audience oriented hedges (14.0, for normalized frequency), followed by accuracy oriented hedges (10.9, for normalized frequency). On the whole, it is found that about 44.1 hedges in every 10,000 words are either directly or indirectly transferred from STs, while about 25.8 hedges in every 10,000 words come from *substitution* or *addition*.

Second, as with interpreting, the raw and normalized frequencies of 'equivalence' surpass those of 'shift' cases across all functional categories of hedges in translated texts. However, it was found that the frequencies of 'shift' cases are only very minimal, most of these falling into the

Table 3 'Equivalence' and 'shift' cases in interpreted versus translated texts[a]

	Accuracy oriented		Speaker/writer oriented		Audience/reader oriented		Total (100%)	
	Equivalence	Shift	Equivalence	Shift	Equivalence	Shift	Equivalence	Shift
Interpreting	407	220	66	17	418	283	891	520
	(20.2)	(10.9)	(3.3)	(0.8)	(20.7)	(14.0)	(44.1)	(25.8)
	28.8%	15.6%	4.7%	1.2%	29.6%	20.1%	63.1%	36.9%
Translation	373	22	23	2	10	1	406	25
	(14.6)	(0.9)	(0.9)	(0.08)	(0.4)	(0.04)	(15.9)	(1.0)
	86.5%	5.1%	5.3%	0.5%	2.3%	0.2%	94.2%	5.8%

[a]In each column, the raw frequency is followed by its normalized frequency per 10,000 words in parenthesis

accuracy oriented category (0.9, for normalized frequency). In general, about 15.9 hedges in every 10,000 words are either directly or indirectly transferred from STs, while about one hedge in every 10,000 words comes from *substitution* or *addition*.

Third, when compared with translated texts, interpreted texts surpass the former in the normalized frequency of 'shift' cases and the percentage they take up in every functional category. In total, roughly 63.1% of hedges belong to 'equivalence' cases in interpreted texts while, in translated texts, 'equivalence' cases account for as much as 94.2%. On the other hand, while only 5.8% of hedges in the translation corpus are 'shift' cases, about 36.9% of hedges in interpreted texts are shifts from the STs.

To summarize, the above results indicate that, on the one hand, 'equivalence' cases outnumber 'shift' cases markedly in both interpreted and translated texts in the use of hedges. On the other hand, 'shift' cases in interpreted texts exceed their counterparts in translated texts markedly, particularly in audience oriented and accuracy oriented categories.

5 Norms and Norm-Taking in Chinese Government Press Conference Interpreting

Since translational norms 'refer to regularities of translation behaviour within a specific sociocultural situation' (Baker 2009: 189), they can be examined by 'identifying regular patterns of translation, including types of strategies that are typically opted for by the translators' (Baker 2009: 191). The patterns of interpreters' manipulation of hedges we have identified above serve as a solid basis for our inquiry into interpreting norms in Chinese government press conferences. In fact, these regular choices by interpreters reveal their compliance with certain interpreting norms, either consciously or subconsciously, that operate in the particular context they situate. Besides, studies in linguistics have suggested that discourses produced in our society, including interpreting, are also subject to various linguistic norms or social expectations on language use. Consequently, the interpreted speeches, as a special type of social discourse, are inevitably subject to various linguistic norms in addition to interpreting norms. The following sections are devoted to discussing these norms by exploiting extra-textual sources as a complement to the above results of textual analysis.

5.1 Linguistic Norms

As revealed in linguistics, particularly pragmatics, there is a set of rules or norms operating in society regarding how language is expected to be used in contexts. As for the use of hedges, their main functions, defined earlier in Sect. 3, suggest the existence of such linguistic norms as 'accuracy' and 'politeness' (corresponding to content motivated and audience motivated hedges, respectively).

In pragmatics, Grice (1975: 45) proposed that interlocutors tend to follow certain conventions in daily conversation, known as the 'cooperative principle', in order to carry out their communication successfully. Particularly, the Quality Maxim under the cooperative principle states that people should not say something they believe to be false, or for which they lack adequate evidence. However, if people do need to express something about which they are not sure, they tend to take proper linguistic measures to mark their uncertainty or their unwillingness to make full commitment. Accuracy oriented and speaker oriented hedges (both as content motivated) are useful linguistic resources available to the speaker to meet the Quality Maxim requirement in conversation. In other words, their use in context suggests a speaker's attempt to comply with the 'accuracy' norm as stated in the Quality Maxim.

In addition, studies in pragmatics also suggest that people are generally expected to show politeness and respect to their conversational partners, in order to accomplish their communicative goals. For instance, Leech (1983: 131) proposed the Politeness Principle, which is further divided into six maxims, to summarize the requirements for politeness in conversation. Among the maxims, the Tact Maxim requires a speaker to minimize the cost to others; the Approbation Maxim, to minimize dispraise of others; and the Agreement Maxim, to minimize disagreement between self and others. Audience oriented hedges, as we have defined above, can serve to mitigate the illocutionary force of a speech act to show deference, modesty, or respect to the hearer, fulfilling the requirement for politeness. Furthermore, in Brown and Levinson's (1987) face theory, hedges are also regarded as an important means for achieving both positive and negative politeness.

Backed up by the above studies, it can be argued that the regular choice of hedges in (interpreted) discourse may be the result of the impact of such linguistic norms as 'accuracy' and 'politeness'. Hedges of different functional categories can be aptly used (by interpreters) to adhere to these norms for successful (inter-cultural) communication. For the present study, interpreters' compliance with such linguistic norms will be discussed later with reference to the regular pattern in their choice of hedges.

5.2 Professional Norms of Interpreting

As with any profession that has its own norms of practice, interpreting has also formed its own distinctive norms in its evolution into an independent profession. For example, some (inter)national organizations of interpreting have formulated a number of normative statements on interpreters' professional standards and codes of conduct. Admittedly, these professional norms of interpreting can exert their influence on interpreters in different ways through a number of means, such as classroom teaching, interpreting textbooks or training manuals, senior interpreters or trainers' comments and their deeds, all of which may find their way into interpreters' modes of practice. A few commonly accepted professional norms can be instantly identified by glancing through the meta-textual materials on interpreting. Among these normative statements, a few are relevant to the present study, including 'faithfulness', 'neutrality', and 'completeness'.

One particular instance is that of the International Association of Conference Interpreters (AIIC). In its 'Practical guide for professional conference interpreters', it has clear requirements for 'faithfulness' and 'completeness' on the part of interpreters, in order 'to communicate the speaker's intended messages as accurately, faithfully, and completely as possible' (AIIC 2017). In other words, interpreters are not expected to deviate from the original meaning, or to add or delete anything from the source contents arbitrarily. So, if 'shifts' occur in interpreting for no obligatory reason, this would run counter to these professional norms. In line with the AIIC, the requirement of 'faithfulness' is also proposed by the Translators Association of China in its Specification for Translation Service, which demands that translators render faithfully the ST into the TT. It is worth noting that 'faithfulness' here, which concerns the relation between STs and TTs, is defined differently from the 'accuracy' norm introduced above, which only concerns expressions in the TT alone. In addition to the faithfulness requirement, statements on 'neutrality' can also be found in the codes made by a few professional organizations. For example, in its Code of Professional Conduct, the British Institute of Translation and Interpreting (ITI) asks its members to 'carry out all work entrusted to them with complete impartiality' (ITI 2016), a duty which should not be impaired by their own interests of any kind. This implies that interpreters must not take sides between the two conversational parties when providing services.

In fact, these metadiscourses on interpreters' professional behaviour and ethical expectations can be found in a number of international and local professional interpreting organizations. It can be assumed that these general norms of interpreting tend to be observed by each interpreter, if he does not want to sacrifice his professional fame, or even jeopardize his professional survival. After all, the breaking of these professional norms for no plausible reason may come at a cost of their identity as a professional. If an interpreter consistently follows the code of conduct, the chances are that these professional norms will gradually be internalized over the course of their career.

5.3 Institutional Norms in Interpreting for Chinese Government Press Conferences

The fact that all interpreters for the Chinese government press conferences are staff (i.e. civil servants from the Department of Translation and Interpreting [DTI] of the Chinese Ministry of Foreign Affairs) defines their practice as a type of institutional translation (or interpreting). The term 'institutional translation', which was first introduced into translation studies by Mossop (1988), refers to translations that are determined by the goals of the translating institutions that produce them. For institutional translation, unlike individual freelance translation, there is always 'an external goal which predetermines participants' roles and influences turn-taking, power relations, footing, topic selection, and so on', as in institutional interaction (Sandrelli 2012: 136). Hence, interpreters in an institutional context are not only professionals in the general sense, but also agents carrying out the institutional practice for institutional goals (see Kang 2009: 144) on a routinized basis. As a result, institutional norms would also find their way into regulating interpreters' behaviour in addition to the professional norms of interpreting in general. As for interpreters from the DTI, these institutional norms influence interpreters' practices, textual choices and their views of interpreting by means of institutional training, collective learning, and institutional rules and regulations (see Wang 2013). For instance, as suggested by the ex-director of the DTI, Shi (2009: 12), 'all translators and interpreters have received formal institutional training of translation/interpreting as well as political studies' before they are assigned any tasks. And these institutional interpreters are expected to conform to institutional requirements in their performance (Ren 2000).

These institutional norms of DTI are discernible from in-house interpreters' own reflections or comments elicited from interviews with expert interpreters. Of particular relevance to this study includes 'loyalty', 'faithfulness', and 'taking a firm stand and exerting subjective initiative' as gatekeepers. For instance, Enlai Zhou, the first premier and foreign minister of the People's Republic of China, once pointed out that 'an interpreter is not just a mechanical sound conduit...but should demonstrate his/her personal awareness and initiative in interpreting' and 'a qualified interpreter should be able to correct the expressions (of a speaker) where they are logically, lexically or syntactically inappropriate' (Shi 2009: 10, my translation). In other words, interpreters are required consciously to defend the government's stance in foreign exchanges. This instruction has been strictly followed by interpreters from the DTI until now. For this purpose, in-house interpreters are required to familiarize themselves with government speakers' intentions and to learn foreign policies, and to 'improve their political awareness through regular discussions and learnings' (Shi 2009: 10, my translation). This clearly indicates that the institutional norms of the DTI require interpreters to be loyal to government speakers, rather than to other participants of communicative events. Besides loyalty, the literature also reveals that faithfulness to the ST is listed by the institution as the paramount principle for the in-house interpreters who service Chinese government press conferences (e.g. Ren 2000; Shi 2009).

5.4 Norm-Taking by Interpreters

Interpreting—a complex interactional activity that involves two languages and three parties—is governed by a variety of norms, as we have noted above. 'An interpreter's on-site behavior is subject to a set of internal and external factors, and his interpreting performance is the result of the combined effect of these multiple factors' (Wang 2013: 78). Though articulated clearly in both professional and institutional norms, it is unlikely that faithfulness will always be taken as the only norm in interpreting; rather, other norms may find their way into interpreters' performance to a greater or lesser extent. Thus, when a set of norms act on the same discourse practice, they have to compete for priority from time to time instead of coexisting with each other in a peaceful way. In this process, conflicts, or even mutual exclusion, may be triggered between different types of norms. The result of their competition is that a certain norm prevails over other norms for a certain discourse choice at a given time. This competition continues in a dynamic way until all the choices are made at a communicative event.

With respect to the current study of interpreting behaviour, conflicts or competition between different types of norms is also evident. For example, though the professional norms of interpreting generally ask interpreters to be 'neutral' when providing services, the institutional norms of the DTI require interpreters to take sides and be loyal to government speakers. Even so, when a disagreement or a criticism is expressed by government speakers, while linguistic norms ask interpreters to be polite, the professional norms of interpreting require interpreters to remain faithful to the original meaning. Depending on whether an interpreter prioritizes their role as a mediator (when politeness and interpersonal harmony are cherished) or as a professional (when faithfulness to the ST is valued), the result of this conflict between norms may be different. Apart from norms from different sources, norms from the same source may also produce conflicts at a given time. Noticeably, the institutional norms of 'faithfulness' may be set against 'exerting subjective initiative' for gate-keeping, at times. For example, when an ST expression is identified as an error or a criticism by an interpreter, they may choose to correct or mitigate it, or to keep it intact. Interpreters' stance leads them to prioritize one particular norm at the expense of other norms when such conflicts arise. Despite the intricacies involved, interpreters' preference for particular norms can be identified by investigating their regular patterns of choices in interpreting with the aid of a corpus.

As for the patterns of hedges in interpreting, the following inferences can be made: first, if interpreters choose 'direct transfer' or 'indirect transfer' (i.e. 'equivalence' cases) of hedges, this suggests that they give priority to the 'faithfulness' norm. Second, if interpreters choose 'substitution' or 'addition' (i.e. 'shift' cases) of hedges, this indicates that the institutional norm of 'exerting subjective initiative' takes precedence over 'faithfulness', which also implies that the institutional norm of 'loyalty' to government speakers is prioritized, as interpreters are manipulating hedges for certain institutional purposes. Third, if interpreters choose substitution or addition of accuracy oriented hedges, this denotes that the 'accuracy' norm is preferred, in order to render the TTs in a linguistically more accurate way. Fourth, if interpreters choose substitution or addition of audience oriented hedges, this shows that the 'politeness' norm is prioritized in order to render the TTs in a more polite way.

The results of the analysis of interpreters' hedges reveals that: first, in Chinese government interpreting and translation, 'faithfulness' is given top priority by both interpreters and translators, which is demonstrated by the fact that 63.1 and 94.2% of hedges in interpreted and translated texts, respectively, are either directly or indirectly transferred from the ST. Second, the linguistic norm of 'politeness' is preferred by interpreters following the 'faithfulness' norm, supported by the fact that those audience oriented hedges that account for 20.1% of all hedges in the interpreted texts are from optional shifts made by interpreters. Third, the linguistic norm of 'accuracy' is also preferred by interpreters, confirmed by the fact that those accuracy oriented hedges that account for about 15.6% of all hedges in the interpreted texts are from optional shifts. Fourth, the above results also reveal the prominent effect of the institutional norms of 'exerting subjective initiative' and 'loyalty' to government speakers in interpreting, manifested as about 36.9% of all hedges, are from optional shifts by interpreters. Lastly, the impact of norms other than 'faithfulness' is minimal in translated texts, as only 5.8% of all hedges with a very low raw frequency are from optional shifts.

6 Conclusion

Exploiting both textual and extra-textual sources, this study probes types of norms and norm-taking in interpreting for Chinese government press conferences by investigating the regular pattern of hedges with the aid of a transcribed corpus. To better identify the distinctive patterns of interpreting, this study is further complemented with a comparative analysis of the translated texts of Chinese government Work Reports. The study ultimately argues that different types of norms exert their influence on interpreters' choice of hedges and compete for priority dynamically. Specifically, the 'faithfulness' norm is prioritized both by interpreters and by translators of Chinese political discourse. Following this, the linguistic norms of 'politeness' and 'accuracy' are also valued by interpreters. Nevertheless, it is also found that the institutional norm of 'loyalty' to government speakers is closely adhered to by interpreters. However, 'faithfulness' seems to be dominant in translators' choice of hedges in the translated texts, with the impact of other norms almost unnoticeable. The results of this study contribute to a more profound understanding of interpreting practice in the Chinese context and also bring useful insights for interpreting quality assessment in the future. In addition, the descriptive approach adopted in this study can also serve as a reference for further empirical inquiries into norms in interpreting studies.

Appendix

List of hedge candidates examined in the present study

about
allegation
allegedly
almost
apparent
apparently
appear
approximately
argue
around
assume
assumption
at least
attempt
basically
belief
believe
broadly
can
chance
claim
comparatively
conceivably
conjecture
contention
could
deduce
doubt
doubtful
essentially
estimate
estimation
expect
expectation
fair
fairly
fear
feel
formally
frequent
frequently
generally
guess
hypothesize
hypothetically
idea
ideally
imply
impossible
improbable
in general
inconceivable
indicate
infer
interpret
interpretation
kind of
largely
likelihood
likely
mainly
maintain
may
maybe
might
more or less
mostly
nearly
normally
occasionally
often
on the whole
opinion
ought
partially
partly
perceive
perhaps
perspective
plausible
plausibly
possibility
possible
possibly
postulate
presumable
presumably
presume
pretty
probability
probable
probably
propose
quite
rare
rarely
rather
reckon
relative
relatively
reportedly
roughly
seem
seemingly
seldom
should
slight
slightly
somehow
sometimes
somewhat
sort of
speculate
speculation
suggest
superficially
suppose
supposedly
surmise
suspect
technically
tend to
tendency
theoretically
think
to my knowledge
to…extent
typical
typically
uncertain
uncertainly
uncertainty
unclear
unclearly
unlikely
unsure
usually
view
virtually
would

References

AIIC. (2017). *Practical Guide for Professional Conference Interpreters*. https://aiic.net/page/628/practical-guide-for-professional-conference-interpreter/lang/1. Last accessed 25 August 2018.

Baker, M. (2009). Norms. In M. Baker & G. Saldanha (Eds.), *Routledge Encyclopedia of Translation Studies* (2nd ed., pp. 189–193). London: Routledge.

Brown, P., & Levinson, S. (1987). *Politeness: Some Universals in Language Usage*. Cambridge: Cambridge University Press.

Gile, D. (1999). Norms in Research on Conference Interpreting: A Response to Theo Hermans and Gideon Toury. In C. Schaffner (Ed.), *Translation and Norms*. Clevedon: Multilingual Matters.

Gile, D. (2009). *Basic Components for Interpreter and Translator Training* (Rev. ed.). Amsterdam/Philadelphia: John Benjamins.

Grice, H. P. (1975). Logic and Conversation. In P. Cole & J. L. Morgan (Eds.), *Syntax and Semantics 3: Speech Acts*. New York: Academic Press.

Harris, B. (1990). Norms in Interpretation. *Target, 2*(1), 115–119.

Holmes, J. (1986). Functions of *You Know* in Women's and Men's Speech. *Language in Society, 15*(1), 1–21.

Holmes, J. (1988). Doubt and Certainty in ESL Textbooks. *Applied Linguistics, 9*(1), 21–44.

Hu, K., & Tao, Q. (2012). Syntactic Operational Norms of Press Conference Interpreting (Chinese–English) (in Chinese). *Foreign Language Teaching and Research, 5*, 738–750.

Hyland, K. (1996a). Talking to the Academy: Forms of Hedging in Science Research Articles. *Written Communication, 13*(2), 251–281.

Hyland, K. (1996b). Writing Without Conviction? Hedging in Science Research Articles. *Applied Linguistics, 17*(4), 433–454.

Hyland, K. (2005). *Metadiscourse*. London: Continuum.

ITI. (2016). *ITI Code of Professional Conduct*. https://www.iti.org.uk/attachments/article/154/Code%20of%20Professional%20Conduct%2029%2010%202016.pdf. Last accessed 25 August 2018.

Kang, J.-H. (2009). Institutional Translation. In M. Baker & G. Saldanha (Eds.), *Routledge Encyclopedia of Translation Studies* (pp. 141–145). Abingdon: Routledge.

Leech, G. (1983). *Principles of Pragmatics*. London: Longman.

Mossop, B. (1988). Translating Institutions: A Missing Factor in Translation Theory. *TTR, 1*(2), 65–71.

Munday, J. (1998). A Computer-Assisted Approach to the Analysis of Translation Shifts. *Meta, 43*(4), 542–556.

Namsaraev, V. (1997). Hedging in Russian Academic Writing in Sociological Texts. In R. Markkanen & H. Schröder (Eds.), *Hedging and Discourse: Approaches to the Analysis of a Pragmatic Phenomenon in Academic Texts* (pp. 64–79). Berlin/New York: Walter de Gruyter.

Ren, X. (2000). On Flexibility in Diplomatic Interpreting (in Chinese). *Chinese Translators Journal, 5,* 40–44.

Sandrelli, A. (2012). Introducing FOOTIE (football in Europe): Simultaneous Interpreting in Football Press Conferences. In F. S. Sergio & C. Falbo (Eds.), *Breaking Ground in Corpus-Based Interpreting Studies.* Bern: Peter Lang.

Seleskovitch, D. (1977). Take Care of the Sense and the Sounds Will Take Care of Themselves or Why Interpreting Is Not Tantamount to Translating Languages. *The Incorporated Linguist, 16,* 27–33.

Shi, Y. (2009). Diplomatic Translation in 60 Years (in Chinese). *Chinese Translators Journal, 5,* 9–12.

Shlesinger, M. (1989). Extending the Theory of Translation to Interpretation: Norms as a Case in Point. *Target, 1*(1), 111–115.

Sun, T. (2014). *Interpreting China: Interpreters' Mediation of Government Press Conferences in China.* Beijing: Foreign Language Teaching and Research Press.

Toury, G. (1978). The Nature and Role of Norms in Literary Translation. In J. S. Holmes, J. Lambert, & R. van den Broeck (Eds.), *Literature and Translation: New Perspectives in Literary Studies* (pp. 83–100). Leuven: ACCO.

Toury, G. (1995). *Descriptive Translation Studies and Beyond.* Amsterdam/Philadelphia: John Benjamins.

Varttala, T. (2001). *Hedging in Scientifically Oriented Discourse: Exploring Variation According to Discipline and Intended Audience* (Unpublished PhD thesis). University of Tampere, Tampere.

Wang, B. (2012). A Descriptive Study of Norms in Interpreting: Based on the Chinese-English Consecutive Interpreting Corpus of Chinese Premier Press Conferences. *Meta, 57*(1), 198–212.

Wang, B. (2013). *A Descriptive Study of Norms in Interpreting: Based on the Analysis of a Corpus of On-Site Interpreting* (in Chinese). Beijing: Foreign Language Teaching and Research Press.

Corpus-based Research on Style and Equivalence

Exploring the Roles of Semantic Prosody and Semantic Preference for Achieving Cross-Language Equivalence: A Corpus-based Contrastive Analysis of Translation Pairs in English and Chinese

Xiaohong Li and Naixing Wei

1 Introduction

Since the early 1990s, the concept of semantic prosody has been a topic of central importance in corpus linguistics (e.g. Bednarek 2008; Hunston 2002; Louw 1993; Partington 2004; Sinclair 1991; Stewart 2010; Stubbs 2001). Although semantic prosody has been widely discussed monolingually—in English, in particular—it has also been brought into close connection with the study of equivalence across languages (Berber-Sardinha 2000; Dam-Jensen and Zethsen 2007; Stewart 2009; Tognini-Bonelli 2002; Xiao and McEnery 2006, among many others). Semantically, semantic prosody is a property of meaning prevailing in context as a result of lexicogrammatical co-selections and,

X. Li (✉)
Shanghai Ocean University, Shanghai, China
e-mail: xh_li@shou.edu.cn; 13371896151@163.com

N. Wei
Beihang University, Beijing, China

K. Hu and K. H. Kim (eds.), *Corpus-based Translation and Interpreting Studies in Chinese Contexts*, Palgrave Studies in Translating and Interpreting,
https://doi.org/10.1007/978-3-030-21440-1_5

pragmatically, it reveals the hidden attitudinal meaning and communicative purpose of a speaker or a writer (Louw 1993; Sinclair 1996; Wei 2011).

Semantic prosody has been variously explored in recent corpus-based contrastive linguistic studies that witnessed a shift of focus from identifying equivalents at the single-word level to exploring equivalence with regard to the lexicogrammatical pattern of words; that is, what Sinclair (1996) calls 'extended units of meaning' (EUM), which involves the core word(s), collocation, colligation, semantic preference, and semantic prosody. This shift is attributed to the rapid adoption of corpus linguistics in translation studies, which makes it possible for collocational, colligational, and semantic preferential profiles of words to be captured, and the correspondence in terms of form and meaning to be assessed. In this regard, semantic prosody serving as the function of an EUM has received increasing attention in rating cross-language equivalents.

Drawing on Sinclair's (1996) framework of EUM, Tognini-Bonelli (2002) addresses 'functionally complete units of meaning' by examining correspondence at the levels of semantic preference and semantic prosody, while Partington (1998) finds, through the comparative analysis of the collocational behaviour and co-texts of words in English and Italian, that perfect equivalents are somewhat rare. Xiao and McEnery (2006), who carry out a detailed contrastive analysis of semantic preferences and prosodies of near synonyms across English and Chinese, argue that collocational behaviour and semantic prosodies of presumed equivalents are unpredictable.

Contrastive linguistic studies of semantic prosody have revealed the important role of semantic prosody in achieving cross-language equivalence, as Stewart (2009: 29) says: 'semantic prosody must be seen as a reality that translators are required to address, otherwise important source text elements will be left unaccounted for'. There are, however, issues that remain to be tackled further.

In the literature, there are two approaches to the typology of semantic prosody, one being the binary good–bad, positive–negative division (e.g. Louw 1993; Partington 1998), and the other being the tripartite labels including positive, negative, and neutral (e.g. Hunston 2007; Stubbs 1995). While Morley and Partington (2009) argue that the good–bad distinction lies at the heart of semantic prosody, Hunston (2007) proposes that semantic prosody cannot be reducible to a simple good–bad division, for this prevents observers from perceiving possibly different interpretations of attitude. This chapter follows the triple division of describing semantic prosody at the macro-level and also provides specific functions. In assessing correspondence at the level of semantic prosody, prosodic strength will be introduced, serving as a useful criterion for rating cross-language equivalence.

Another issue is concerned with the transference of semantic prosody. Multi-disciplinary studies show that semantic prosody is discipline- and domain-specific (Hunston 2007; Nelson 2006). Hunston (2007) demonstrates that the verb 'cause' implies something undesirable, but its prosody becomes neutral in scientific texts. Through a stylistic lens, Louw (1993) finds that a divergence from a normal prosody can be the exploitation of prosody to fulfil a special communicative purpose, such as irony. Morley and Partington (2009) explain the concept of prosodic clash where the expectations of a normal prosody are overturned, exploited or, in Hoey's (2005) term, 'switched off'.

The transference of semantic prosody across disciplines or domains is beyond the discussion of this chapter, but we will argue that shifts in semantic prosody are not only dependent on text types, but also closely related with patterns of co-selection. One of the crucial observations of cross-language researchers is that expectations of semantic prosody are not always fully conscious for translators (Partington 1998; Stewart 2009). In this regard, the exploited or switched-off prosody in the cross-linguistic context may be more complex and needs further exploration.

Against this background, this study explores the complex relationships between patterns of co-selection and cross-language equivalence by analysing features of the four types of Sinclairian co-selection: collocation, colligation, semantic preference, and semantic prosody.[1]

[1]Due to the complexity and variability of colligational patterns in Chinese, colligational profiles of a node word will be given a brief description in this study, but a systemic investigation of the inter-relationship between syntactic patterns and cross-language equivalence calls for more efforts in future studies.

More attention will be given to the changes of meaning and function brought about by changes of co-selection patterns in this contrastive study of cross-language equivalence.

This study begins by looking at presumed translation pairs extracted from a bi-directional English–Chinese parallel corpus—the Shanghai Jiao Tong University (SJTU) Parallel Corpus—before analysing the features of collocation, colligation, semantic preference, and semantic prosody of each translation pair in comparable corpora (the Modern Chinese Corpus: MCC) and (the British National Corpus: BNC). Three important components of an EUM, semantic prosody, semantic preference, and collocates will be examined in detail for their roles in establishing cross-language equivalence.

We ultimately argue that a word is habitually involved in more than one pattern; that each pattern is associated with a particular semantic prosody; and that cross-language equivalence resides in corresponding patterns of co-selection, rather than word-to-word equivalents. We will also show that the alteration of one component in a pattern may affect cross-language equivalence to varying degrees.

Section 2 defines analytical concepts and describes the research method. In Sect. 3, co-selection patterns of translation pairs will be analysed in some depth, whereby phraseological patterns will be formulated and pattern equivalence established. A brief summary of pattern equivalence will be provided in Sect. 4. Section 5 concentrates on discussing the role of semantic prosody, semantic preference, and collocates in establishing cross-language equivalence. The major findings and implications will be discussed in Sect. 6.

2 Research Method

This section, first, briefly explains the main concepts and terms needed for subsequent discussions. After an introduction of the corpora and corpus tools used in the study, we will propose the analytical procedure, in which typical patterns between English and Chinese will be identified and contrasted.

2.1 Analytical Concepts

The key concepts in this study include semantic prosody, prosodic strength, prosodic norm, semantic preference, collocation, and phraseological pattern. In line with Sinclair (1996), 'semantic prosody' refers to the attitudinal meaning expressed by the interplay between a node word (the core), colligation, collocation, and semantic preference, which essentially indicates the communicative purpose of a speaker or a writer. Semantic prosody is essentially 'concerned with broad aspects of meaning, including attitudes, tactics and pragmatics' (Sinclair 2010: 45). In light of this, when discussing a semantic prosody we use 'attitudinal meaning' and 'semantic prosody' interchangeably. In this study, the description of a semantic prosody involves both a specific function and an overall attitude; that is, a positive, negative, or neutral prosody. Whether an attitudinal meaning is generally favourable or unfavourable can be measured by an index of prosodic strength, which can be obtained through a simple calculation, as shown in the formulas $PS = F_{pos}/F_N$ and $PS = F_{neg}/F_N$.

Here, PS refers to prosodic strength, F_{pos} and F_{neg}, respectively, stand for the occurrence of positive and negative prosodies associated with a pattern, and F_N is the total frequency of this pattern identified in a corpus. For instance, one pattern of 夺取 *duoqu* occurs 30 times in MCC, and 23 out of the total 30 instances deliver a negative prosody. In this case, $F_{neg}=23$, $F_N=30$, and $PS=23/30\approx0.77$. Thus, the prosodic strength index (PSI) is 0.77, which means that the probability for this pattern to deliver a negative prosody is higher than that of the positive one. Prosodic strength is 'of practical value to assessing degrees of equivalence between translation equivalents' (Wei and Li 2014: 109).

Another important concept in describing semantic prosody is the prosodic norm, which Morley and Partington (2009: 148) describe as the 'background or default prosody'. The proposal of the prosodic norm is attributed to the recurrent and conventional use of language where a given pattern of co-selection is habitually associated with a particular semantic prosody. This prosody that predominates over the pattern can be regarded as the norm against which counter-examples are possible to detect and discern. To discuss examples that run counter to the norm, we incorporate the PSI into the recognition of the prosodic norm. In practical terms, when the PSI of a positive attitudinal meaning is higher than that of a negative one, the prosodic norm is recognized as positive and any instance of a negative prosody is regarded as divergence from the prosodic norm. Relevant discussions will be made in Sect. 5.

In this study, words from the same semantic set that frequently co-occur with a node word are referred to as 'collocates'. The term 'collocation' refers to the relationship a lexical item has with words that appear more than twice in the context. Bublitz (1998: 16) notes that there exist cases 'not of word-to-word collocation but of word-to-class, or rather word-to-semantic-class-of-word collocation'. This last kind of collocational relationship is exactly what is referred to as 'semantic preference', which has set off a heated discussion in corpus-based studies of phraseology and is also a main concern in the present study. In this study, by 'semantic preference' we mean 'the restriction of regular co-occurrence to items which share a semantic feature' (Sinclair 2004: 142).

'Phraseological pattern' in this study refers to the co-selection of a node word with semantic preference and semantic prosody. The identification of a pattern follows the same step of identifying an EUM (Sinclair 1996), with a close observation of collocation, colligation, semantic preference, and prosody, but the representation of a pattern in this study highlights the co-occurring semantic features and the specific attitudinal meaning, shown as follows:

([semantic feature]$_{\textbf{PREF}}$) node [semantic feature]$_{\textbf{PREF}}$ ⟹ [attitudinal meaning]$_{\textbf{PROS}}$

In the pattern, the semantic feature in square brackets represents semantic preference, shortened as PREF. As is often the case, a node word may demonstrate more than one semantic preference in its vicinity. The semantic preference in parentheses means that this semantic set occasionally co-occurs with the node and that it is not an inherent component of the pattern. The arrow pointing to an attitudinal meaning indicates that semantic preference contributes to the reading of a prosodic meaning, and PROS stands for the semantic prosody associated with the pattern. For instance, the Chinese word 夺取 *duoqu* is found to be embedded in this pattern:

([intention]$_{PREF}$) 夺取 *duoqu* [victory/success]$_{PREF}$ $\Longrightarrow$ [desiring to achieve]$_{PROS}$

To the left of the node verb, there is an occasional semantic preference of 'intention', which is realized by different grammatical words, such as 为 *wei* (for the purpose of), 要 *yao* (intend to) and 去 *qu* (to). To the right of the node, a noticeable semantic preference of 'victory/success' is detected in a strong colligation of *V n*. Both the occasional and inherent semantic preferences contribute to recognizing a specific attitudinal meaning of 'desiring to achieve' and, on the whole, the pattern delivers a favourable semantic prosody. Section 3 will detail the description of the pattern of each word under study.

2.2 Corpora

This study employs two general corpora, the BNC and the MCC, as comparable corpora. We use the written part of the BNC, which is available at http://corpus.bye.edu/bnc/. It comprises 90 million running words and consists of books (58%), newspapers (30%), published and unpublished articles (10%), and articles for oral use (2%) (see http://www.natcorp.ox.ac.uk, for details). The core part of the MCC, commonly referred to as the Main Corpus of MCC, is composed of texts from books, newspapers, and journals. This corpus, with 20 million running Chinese characters, covers the topics of the humanities and social sciences (50%), natural sciences (30%), and miscellany (20%). These two general corpora will be used for exploring patterns in English and Chinese with authentic instances of lexical words extracted and compared.

The study also employs a parallel corpus to posit presumed translation equivalents: the SJTU Parallel Corpus. As a bi-directional English–Chinese parallel corpus with 3,620,790 running English words and 5,362,748 running Chinese characters, it consists of three subcorpora, each covering different topics: politics, science and technology, and the humanities (see Wei 2011, for more information). Translation pairs can be extracted from the parallel corpus for further contrastive analysis.

2.3 Translation Pairs

This study focuses on investigating pattern equivalence for three Chinese verbs: 夺取 *duoqu*, 助长 *zhuzhang*, and 平息 *pingxi*.

We start with translation pairs extracted from the parallel corpus, which shows the translation equivalents to be of a complex one-to-many matching relationship. For instance, 夺取 *duoqu* in SJTU Parallel Corpus is found to correspond to eight English equivalents in different contexts, including *seize*, *wrest*, *capture*, *take over*, *accomplish*, *achieve*, *win*, and *take*. We confine ourselves to the most typical translation pairs for a detailed analysis of their respective collocational and preferential profiles and semantic prosodies. In this respect, as a reference criterion we adopt Altenberg's (1999: 254) Mutual Correspondence (MC) to posit typical translation pairs for subsequent investigation. The formula of calculating MC is $MC = [(A_t + B_t)/(A_s + B_s)] * 100\%$.

Here, respectively, A_t and B_t stand for the frequency of Word A and the frequency of Word B in texts of the target language and, respectively, A_s and B_s refer to the frequencies of Word A and Word B in the source language texts. For instance, in the SJTU Parallel Corpus 夺取 *duoqu* and *SEIZE* occur, respectively, 35 times in the Chinese source texts and 37 times in the English source texts: $A_s = 35$, $B_s = 37$. If 夺取 *duoqu* is translated as *SEIZE* 16 times and *SEIZE* as 夺取 *duoqu* twice, then $A_t = 16$, $B_t = 2$. According to the formula, $MC = (16 + 2) * 100\%/(35 + 37) = 25\%$.

Since the MC value provides quantitative information on the translatability of words in the two different languages, the MC value was used as the ad hoc baseline for choosing word-to-word translation pairs. For practical reasons, our analysis focused on the translation pairs with the highest MC values of all the pairs under observation. The respective ad hoc equivalents of the three Chinese words are set up because their MC values are higher than those of other translation candidates. Table 1 shows three selected translation pairs with their respective MC values.

Table 1 Translation pairs with MC values

Translation pairs	MC (%)
夺取 *duoqu* versus *SEIZE*	25.0
助长 *zhuzhang* versus *FUEL*	42.9
平息 *pingxi* versus *ASSUAGE*	25.0

Note that the English verbs in capitals stand for lemmas, including all forms of inflections. For instance, *SEIZE* covers the forms of *seize*, *seizes*, *seized*, and *seizing*. The translation pairs shown in Table 1 are presumed equivalents at the single-word level, which is the starting point of the contrastive exploration. Each word will be taken as the node in the corpus-based investigation; the ultimate goal of the analysis is to find patterns of equivalence between the two languages, with the profiles of collocation, semantic preference, and prosody identified and compared.

2.4 Research Procedure

The study follows three procedural steps in its analysis of pattern equivalence. First, translation pairs are selected from the SJTU Parallel Corpus. Second, we turn to the comparable corpora, the MCC and BNC, to examine collocational, preferential, and functional profiles of the translation pairs, with special attention being paid to semantic preference and prosody. The four categories of co-selection—collocation, colligation, semantic preference and semantic prosody—in the model of the EUM (Sinclair 1996) offer keen insights into the pattern behaviour of a node word.

In this study, the most frequent pattern of a word is referred to as the 'major pattern', which is regarded as forming a unit of meaning. The different patterns are the bases for exploring cross-language equivalence. At the same time, PSIs are calculated and a prosodic norm is assigned to a pattern. In doing so, 100 concordances of each word will be extracted from the MCC or the BNC for an in-depth examination and, if the occurrence of a word in a corpus is fewer than 100, all the instances will be retrieved for investigation.

Third, cross-language equivalence will be established based on contrastive information of semantic prosody, semantic preference, and collocational behaviour, and their respective contributions to cross-language equivalence will be discussed in depth.

3 Phraseological Pattern and Pattern Equivalence

In this section, patterns associated with each word under study are identified, first, with collocational and preferential regularities recognized and the semantic prosody captured. We then move on to assessing similarities of patterns in terms of semantic preference and semantic prosody so as to propose pattern equivalence.

3.1 夺取 *duoqu* Versus *SEIZE*

In this part, collocational profiles, preferential profiles, and semantic prosody will be focused on in a detailed and systematic manner so as to identify patterns associated with 夺取 *duoqu* and *SEIZE* so as to arrive at pattern equivalence.

3.1.1 Co-selection Patterns of 夺取 *duoqu* Versus *SEIZE*

An observation of 100 concordances randomly chosen from the MCC shows that a number of nouns occurring to the right of 夺取 *duoqu* serve as the head of the object phrase and that nouns to the left of 夺取 *duoqu* function as the head of the subject phrase. It is found that the head nouns of the object phrase can be roughly arranged into four semantic groups. Recurrent collocates and other one-off co-occurring nouns contribute to the reading of semantic prosodies. The patterns associated with 夺取 *duoqu* are presented in Table 2.

As Table 2 shows, 夺取 *duoqu* is frequently embedded in Pattern 1, which accounts for 37% of the total 100 instances under scrutiny. In this pattern, 夺取 *duoqu* habitually co-occurs with the semantic

Table 2 Patterns and PSI associated with 夺取 *duoqu*

Patterns	PSI
Pattern 1 (37%)[a] ([intention]$_{PREF}$) 夺取 *duoqu* [victory/success]$_{PREF}$ ⟹ [desiring to achieve something]$_{PROS}$	Pos. 1.0
Pattern 2 (30%) ([armed military battle]$_{PREF}$) 夺取 *duoqu* [territories of a sovereign state]$_{PREF}$ ⟹ [wild ambition or determination]$_{PROS}$	Neg. 0.77
Pattern 3 (18%) [men of a social class]$_{PREF}$ 夺取 *duoqu* [power]$_{PREF}$ ⟹ [a tactical plan or a purposeful plot]$_{PROS}$	Pos. 0.63
Pattern 4 (15%) 夺取 *duoqu* [dominant position or competitive advantage]$_{PREF}$ ⟹ [desirable goal]$_{PROS}$	Pos. 0.60

[a]The percentage represents the relative frequency of a pattern in the overall occurrences. For instance, 37% shows that the pattern of 夺取 *duoqu* occurs 37 times in every 100 occurrences

preference 'victory/success', which is realized by a group of noun collocates. Among them, 胜利 *shengli* (victory) and 全胜 *quansheng* (complete victory) can refer to a victory in a military fight, athletic game, or financial competition, while 冠军 *guanjun* (champion), 金牌 *jinpai* (gold medal), and 奖牌 *jiangpai* (medal) denote the highest honour and success in sports games. In addition, 丰收 *fengshou* (harvest) and 高产 *gaochan* (high production), referring to farmers' bumper harvests, are metaphorically used to depict human success in competing with nature.

Immediately to the left of 夺取 *duoqu*, words, such as 为 *wei* (for the purpose of), 要 *yao* (intend to), and 去 *qu* (to), are found to convey the message of a strong intention. Thus, the preference of 'victory/success', coupled with an occasional semantic feature of 'intention', points to a semantic prosody of 'desiring to achieve something'.

We have now arrived at the major pattern of 夺取 *duoqu*, delivering the message that one is ready to achieve success with an unyielding determination. Moreover, this pattern invariably conveys a favourable semantic prosody and the PSI is 1.0. This is explicable because, in universal terms, it is desirable to achieve success and win victory.

Pattern 2, taking up 30% of the total, displays another important lexicogrammatical environment in which 夺取 *duoqu* habitually occurs.

As Table 2 illustrates, 夺取 *duoqu* and the semantic preference 'territories of a sovereign state' co-select. In this co-selection, 夺取土地 *duoqutudi* (seize territory) in the MCC is a frequent collocation, co-occurring 5 times. 夺取 *duoqu* also co-occurs with a group of nouns denoting different territorial places. At the same time, a bundle of lexical items in the vicinity of 夺取 *duoqu* have the semantic feature of 'armed military battle'. These include 反击 *fanji* (counterattack), 作战 *zuozhan* (fight), 战争 *zhanzheng* (war), 战役 *zhanyi* (battle), 战斗 *zhandou* (fighting), 战败 *zhanbai* (suffer a defeat), and 打败 *dabai* (defeat). This semantic preference, together with other expressions of varied forms, can help to discern the implied attitudinal meaning.

One group of the varied expressions, including 侵占 *qinzhan* (invade and occupy), 寻求财富 *xunqiu caifu* (in search of wealth), 吞并 *tunbin* (annex), 野心 *yexin* (wild ambition), 殖民者 *zhiminzhe* (colonist), 列强 *lieqiang* (foreign powers), 疯狂地 *fengkuangde* (crazily), 企图 *qitu* (with evil intention), and 妄图 *wangtu* (try in vain), depict and highlight invaders' evil intention and reinforces a negative prosody of condemnation. Another small group of collocates, including 根据地 *genjudi* (base), 英雄 *yingxiong* (hero), 打倒军阀 *dadao junfa* (overthrow warlords), 打败侵略者 *dabai qinlvezhe* (defeat invaders), 游击战争 *youji zhanzheng* (guerrilla warfare), and 人民战争 *renmin zhanzheng* (people's war), suggest a strong will to take back the invaded territory, which thus enhances a positive prosody of support. Pattern 2 has a negative PSI of 0.77, much higher than the positive PSI of 0.23 (23 out of the total 30 instances deliver a negative prosody and the remaining 7 instances express a positive prosody).

Of the 100 concordances, there are 18 instances where 夺取 *duoqu* co-occurs with a semantic preference of 'power', which is realized by nouns such as 政权 *zhengquan* (political power), 统治权 *tongzhiquan* (ruling power), 皇权 *huangquan* (imperial power), and 权力 *quanli* (power).

The reading of the semantic prosody is primarily dependent on the agent of the action, which is found to be 'man of a particular social class'. In some historical moments, getting power by force on behalf of people may be the last resort in order to overthrow corrupt authorities. On the other hand, getting power for one's own interests is considered a blameable plot. It is found that Pattern 3, taking 夺取 *duoqu* as the core, may express either a positive or negative prosody, with the former showing a PSI of 0.61 and the latter 0.39 (11 out of 18 instances express a favourable attitude and the other 7 instances deliver an unfavourable attitude).

Pattern 4 makes up 15% of the total and, in this pattern, 夺取 *duoqu* co-occurs with nouns such as 优势 *youshi* (advantage), 武器 *wuqi* (weapon), 领先地位 *lingxian diwei* (leading position), 主动权 *zhudongquan* (initiative), 利润 *lirun* (profit), 权益 *quanyi* (interests), and 市场 *shichang* (market). All these nouns point to a preference of 'dominance or advantage in a competitive situation'. Taking into consideration the co-text, we find that 60% of the co-occurrences deliver a favourable attitudinal meaning and thus the PSI is 0.60. This is understandable for the reason that being in a dominant or advantageous position is generally a goal to achieve in all sorts of competitions.

Our observation has shown that 夺取 *duoqu* is associated with four patterns, among which the major pattern accounts for 37%. It is also noticeable that each pattern varies in semantic preference, semantic prosody, and prosodic strength.

Let us turn to the examination of 100 concordances of *SEIZE*. It is found that *SEIZE* most frequently collocates with *opportunity* and *chance* to form the phraseological sequence *SEIZE the (one's) opportunity (chance) of (to)*, making up 23% of the total instances. This sequence, relatively stable in form and meaning, constitutes a single choice in use and thus is embedded in a larger unit of meaning. Apart from this phraseological sequence, the noun collocates as the head of the object phrase, though very varied, and falls approximately into three semantic subsets. Based on the collocational, preferential, and functional regularities in the co-text of *SEIZE*, we arrive at six patterns, which are presented in Table 3.

SEIZE habitually co-occurs with *territory/territories*, *land/lands*, *town/towns*, *city/cities*, and many other different nouns denoting places or areas of sovereignty. At the same time, expressions in the co-text, such as *guerrillas*, *Turkish forces*, *Iran*, *YUGOSLAV army troops*, *army rebels*, *protesters*, and *Fatah guerrillas* suggest a semantic aura of tension, turbulence, or illegitimate actions, helping to deliver and reinforce a semantic

Table 3 Patterns and PSI associated with *SEIZE*

Patterns	PSI
Pattern 1 (19%) ([armed forces]$_{PREF}$) *SEIZE* [places/territories of a sovereign state]$_{PREF}$ ⟹ [opposition]$_{PROS}$	Neg. 1.0
Pattern 2 (17%) ([intention]$_{PREF}$) *SEIZE* [political power]$_{PREF}$ ([armed forces]$_{PREF}$) ⟹ [illegal plots]$_{PROS}$	Neg. 1.0
Pattern 3 (10%) *SEIZE* [dominant or advantageous position]$_{PREF}$ ⟹ [desirable goal]$_{PROS}$	Pos. 0.5/Neg.0.5
Pattern 4 (14%) [illicit properties]$_{PREF}$ BE *seized* by [officers with authority to enforce the law]$_{PREF}$ ⟹ [seriousness]$_{PROS}$	Pos. 0.86
Pattern 5 (9%) [someone]$_{PREF}$ BE *seized* with/by [strong emotions]$_{PREF}$ ⟹ [losing control of reasoning]$_{PROS}$	Neg. 0.78
Pattern 6 (8%) [someone innocent]$_{PREF}$ BE seized by or *SEIZE* [someone innocent]$_{PREF}$ ⟹ [disagreement]$_{PROS}$	Neg. 1.0

prosody of disagreement. As shown in Table 3, *SEIZE* is thus involved in Pattern 1, which accounts for 19% of the total 100 instances. This pattern invariably expresses a negative prosody and the PSI is 1.0.

In Table 3, Pattern 2 of *SEIZE* is composed of the core, an inherent preference 'political power', and two optional preferences. The intimacy between *SEIZE* and *power* is shown by their 17 co-occurrences, accounting for 17% of the concordances. Occasionally, expressions such as *planned to*, *an attempt to*, and *attempting to* occurring to the left of *SEIZE power* point to a slight preference of 'intention'. Beyond this position, another group of expressions have the semantic feature of 'armed forces', which include *army-backed coup*, *bloodless coup*, *coup*, *armed coup*, *anti-democratic forces*, *armed forces*, *the military*, *terroristic conspiracy*, *mercenaries*, and *a group of soldiers*. These semantic preferential profiles serve to build a negative prosody of 'illegal plot'.

In Pattern 3, *SEIZE* and the preference of 'dominance' do not co-select frequently. Moreover, there seems a balance between the favourable and unfavourable semantic prosodies, with a positive PSI of 0.5 and a negative PSI of 0.5.

Pattern 4 expresses that 'illicit properties' are usually taken away by 'someone with authority to enforce the law', such as *police officers*, and thus delivers a prosody of seriousness highlighted in the enforcement of the law. In Pattern 5, *SEIZE* often appears in the phraseological sequence *BE* seized with/by 'strong emotions', implying the disapproval of losing one's control of reasoning. In Pattern 6, *SEIZE* habitually attracts nouns denoting someone who is innocent, including *customer*, *hostages*, *officials*, *officer*, and *prince*. To capture innocent people delivers a sense of disagreement.

3.1.2 Pattern Equivalence Between 夺取 *duoqu* and *SEIZE*

With phraseological patterns identified in the previous section, pattern equivalence is assessed by comparing similarities in preferential profiles and semantic prosody.

We note that in the colligation *V n*, both 夺取 *duoqu* and *SEIZE* co-occur with nouns pointing to the semantic preference 'places of a sovereign state'. The patterns associated with these two verbs show a high probability of delivering a negative prosody. With the semantic and functional resemblance, the Pattern 1 equivalence can be suggested as follows:

Pattern Equivalence 1

([armed military battle]$_{\text{PREF}}$) **夺取 *duoqu*** [territories of a sovereign state]$_{\text{PREF}}$
$\Longrightarrow$ [wild ambition or determination]$_{\text{PROS}}$ Neg. PSI = 0.77
([armed forces]$_{\text{PREF}}$) ***SEIZE*** [places of a sovereign state]$_{\text{PREF}}$
$\Longrightarrow$ [opposition]$_{\text{PROS}}$ Neg. PSI = 1.0

It is also noted that the co-occurrence of *SEIZE* and nouns denoting 'power' bears a marked resemblance to Pattern 3 of 夺取 *duoqu*. In terms of semantic prosody, the pattern associated with *SEIZE* delivers an overwhelmingly negative attitudinal meaning, while Pattern 3 of 夺取 *duoqu*, albeit habitually carrying a positive prosody, also shows a probability of nearly 40% for a negative attitudinal meaning. This means that there exist possibilities for the two patterns to be functionally equivalent.

Pattern Equivalence 2

[men of a social class]$_{PREF}$ **夺取** ***duoqu*** [power]$_{PREF}$
⟹ [a tactical plan or a purposeful plot]$_{PROS}$ Neg. PSI = 0.39 (Pos. PSI = 0.61)
([intention]$_{PREF}$) ***SEIZE*** [political power]$_{PREF}$ ([armed forces])
⟹ [illegal plots]$_{PROS}$ Neg. PSI = 1.0

In an infrequent pattern, *SEIZE* shows similarities with 夺取 *duoqu* in collocations with *weapons* and *initiative*. Despite the lexical overlaps, the co-occurrence of *SEIZE* and the preference 'dominance', with only 10 instances in the BNC, is relatively rarer than is the case of its Chinese counterpart. In the same semantic environment, the patterns of these two verbs exhibit similar probabilities to express a positive semantic prosody, and thus the pattern equivalence is:

Pattern Equivalence 3

夺取 ***duoqu*** [dominant position or competitive advantage]$_{PREF}$
⟹ [desirable goal]$_{PROS}$ Pos. PSI = 0.6
SEIZE [dominant or advantageous position]$_{PREF}$
⟹ [desirable goal]$_{PROS}$ Pos. PSI = 0.5

Two important features of cross-language equivalence are now emerging from the above findings. First, to an extent, there can be collocational overlaps for a word-to-word translation pair, but their semantic preferential profiles normally exhibit complexities for assessing correspondence. For example, although 夺取 *duoqu* and *SEIZE* show similarities in three semantic preferences—'territories', 'power' and 'dominance'—other preferences of the two words differ to varying degrees. More specifically, co-occurring with the semantic preference of 'power', 夺取 *duoqu* regularly expects 'man of a social class' to occur in the preceding co-text, while *SEIZE* attracts 'intention' in its left environment. This leads us to the finding that the inherent semantic preference is obligatory in assessing pattern equivalence, while optional preferences are less critical because pattern equivalence could tolerate differences in semantic sets occurring occasionally around the node.

Second, a pair of pattern equivalences may have the same polarity of semantic prosody, but the prosodic strengths may vary to a greater or lesser extent. For instance, in the Pattern Equivalence 2, when co-occurring with the preference of 'places', the pattern of 夺取 *duoqu* shows a moderately strong negative prosody, with a PSI of 0.77, slightly lower than the index of 1.0 of the negative semantic prosody associated with the pattern of *SEIZE*. However, when co-occurring with the preference of 'power', their respective patterns exhibit markedly different prosodic strengths, with 夺取 *duoqu* associated with a positive PSI of 0.61 and *SEIZE* a very high index of 1.0 of negative semantic prosody. There is nearly a 40% possibility of the prosodic norm of 夺取 *duoqu* being converted to another direction of attitude. Instances that diverge from the norm will be dealt with in more detail in Sect. 1.

3.2 助长 *zhuzhang* Versus *FUEL*

This section deals with proposing pattern equivalence between 助长 *zhuzhang* and *FUEL* by looking at similarities in terms of semantic preference and semantic prosody.

3.2.1 Co-selection Patterns of 助长 *zhuzhang* Versus *FUEL*

Of a total of 95 concordances, 5 nominal uses, and 10 idioms, 80 concordances of 助长 *zhuzhang* in the MCC are examined (instances such as 拔苗助长 *bamiaozhuzhang* and 揠苗助长 *yamiaozhuzhang* 'pull a seedling upward in the mistaken hope of accelerating its growth' are excluded). It is found that 助长 *zhuzhang* habitually occurs in the colligation: *(aux/adv) V (past tense) adj n*. Immediately to the right of 助长 *zhuzhang* is the Chinese character 了 *le*, a perfective aspect marker (Xiao 2010), accounting for 50% of the concordances studied. This indicates that the perfective aspect is an important co-selection of 助长

zhuzhang. To the left, we find a frequent colligation of auxiliaries (e.g. 会 *hui* 'can', 可能 *keneng* 'could') and adverbs (e.g. 徒然 *turan* 'vainly', 大大 *dada* 'enormously', 往往 *wangwang* 'often'). To the right, there is a strong colligation with nouns at the R1, R2, and R3 positions. By taking into account the collocational and preferential profiles, the patterns of 助长 *zhuzhang* together with the PSI are shown in Table 4.

Three noteworthy features emerge from Table 4. First, the central use of 助长 *zhuzhang* lies in the indispensable prosody of 'expressing severity of an evil development' as the negative prosody is associated with each pattern. This means that Chinese native speakers are very likely to relate 助长 *zhuzhang* with a negative attitude and expect this verb to occur in an unpleasant context.

Second, in each pattern the obligatory semantic preference is realized by a colligation *V n* and a variety of lexical selections. In addition, some noun collocates strongly expect pre-noun modifiers to specify the local meanings, and thus the colligation *V n* can be enlarged into *V adj n*. For instance, in Pattern 3 助长 *zhuzhang* habitually co-occurs with the recurrent collocate 气焰 *qiyan* (arrogance) and other one-off collocates, including 势头 *shitou* (momentum), 气势 *qishi* (imposing manner), 声势 *shengshi* (momentum), and 威势 *weishi* (power). These noun collocates refer to the manner or force that keeps a process developing or happening more quickly and forcefully, and the obligatory semantic preference can be termed 'manner/momentum'. This preference

Table 4 Patterns and PSI associated with 助长 *zhuzhang*

Patterns	PSI
Pattern 1 (51%) ([amplification/negation]$_{PREF}$) 助长 *zhuzhang* [tendency/habit]$_{PREF}$ ⟹ [severity]$_{PROS}$	Neg. 0.8
Pattern 2 (20%) ([possibility]$_{PREF}$) 助长 *zhuzhang* [social phenomenon or activities]$_{PREF}$ ⟹ [severity]$_{PROS}$	Neg. 0.62
Pattern 3 (19%) ([amplification]$_{PREF}$) 助长 *zhuzhang* [manner/momentum]$_{PREF}$ ⟹ [severity]$_{PROS}$	Neg. 0.67
Pattern 4 (10%) 助长 *zhuzhang* [pathological/physical/natural phenomenon]$_{PREF}$ ⟹ [severity]$_{PROS}$	Neg. 0.63

seems to be neutral and suggests no clues to the attitudinal meaning. However, these nouns strongly rely on previous modifiers for carrying more semantic information. Some instances of modifier-noun co-occurrences, presented in bold, are shown in Examples (1)–(3):

Example (1)

法西斯意大利的侵略气焰 *faxisi yidali de qinlve qiyan* (the aggression **of fascist Italy**)

Example (2)

敌人的嚣张气焰 *diren de xiaozhang qiyan* (the arrogance **of the enemy**)

Example (3)

殖民侵略的势头 *zhimin qinlve de shitou* (**colonial** aggression)

The above pre-noun modifiers share the same semantic features of 'unjust', 'aggressive', and 'overwhelming'. This contributes to the reading of a negative prosody for 'severe and culpable' because the act of fuelling an unjust or aggressive manner is generally considered as being condemnable.

Third, beyond the colligation *V adj n*, to the left of the node there are several optional preferences, such as 'amplification' and 'possibility', that occasionally accompany 助长 *zhuzhang*. These preferences often serve to reinforce the negative aura in the context and help to discern semantic prosody.

FUEL occurs 5154 times in the BNC. Among 100 concordances randomly selected, 54% denote the basic sense 'to supply power to a vehicle or machine' and the remaining 46% are metaphorical uses. The basic sense of *FUEL* bears no semantic resemblance to 助长 *zhuzhang* whatsoever. In view of this, we confine ourselves to its metaphorical uses and randomly choose another 100 instances for scrutiny.

Concordances show that there is a strong colligation with nouns preceding and following the node verb due to its transitivity. Nouns to the right of *FUEL* account for 53% of the total and, in between, there are many instances of the grammatical classes of determiner and possessive adjective, such as *the*, *a*, *an*, *her*, *his*, and *my*, hence the colligation of *V det/possadj n*. A further examination of semantic preferential and prosodic profiles shows that *FUEL* is associated with four patterns, which are presented in Table 5.

In spite of differences in semantic preference, all four patterns associated with *FUEL* tend to denote a negative semantic prosody of 'severity'. This indicates that native speakers of English are prone to predict *FUEL* to occur in a negative lexicogrammatical environment.

Another noticeable feature lies in the collocational behaviour of *FUEL*. Unlike 助长 *zhuzhang*, the noun collocates of *FUEL* do not show a strong reliance on the pre-noun modifiers to specify their semantic meanings. That is, in the colligation *V n* the noun collocates that point to a semantic preference can suggest an attitudinal meaning in a straightforward way. In Pattern 2, for instance, *FUEL* is found to collocate very frequently with *speculation*, *rumours*, *fear/fears*, *doubt*, *suspicions*, *concern/concerns*, and *apprehension*. This group of nouns has an inherent meaning of 'uncertain or ungrounded belief'. The feeling of gravity is implied by the co-occurrence of *FUEL* and its noun collocates, which indicates that the psychological uncertainty is groundless, widespread, and overwhelming. Pattern 2 is associated with an invariably negative semantic prosody of 'seriousness'.

FUEL is also seen to collocate frequently with nouns expressing 'a confrontation of ideas or actions'. The recurrent collocates include *controversy*, *arguments*, *debate*, *war/wars*, and *conflict*. The co-occurrences constitute Pattern 3 and deliver the message that 'a confrontation of ideas or actions continues and gets worse', and the semantic prosody of 'severity' could be easily perceived.

Table 5 Patterns and PSI associated with *FUEL*

Patterns	PSI
Pattern 1 (35%) *FUEL* [financial or social phenomenon]$_{PREF}$ $\Longrightarrow$ [severity]$_{PROS}$	Neg. 0.63
Pattern 2 (28%) *FUEL* [uncertain/ungrounded belief]$_{PREF}$ $\Longrightarrow$ [seriousness]$_{PROS}$	Neg. 1.0
Pattern 3 (25%) *FUEL* [confrontational ideas/actions]$_{PREF}$ $\Longrightarrow$ [severity]$_{PROS}$	Neg. 0.84
Pattern 4 (12%) *FUEL* [strong emotion/mentality]$_{PREF}$ $\Longrightarrow$ [severity]$_{PROS}$	Neg. 0.67

3.2.2 Pattern Equivalence Between 助长 zhuzhang and FUEL

Having identified different sets of patterns associated with 助长 *zhuzhang* and *FUEL*, we now move on to the exploration of pattern equivalence between them.

Despite variations, 助长 *zhuzhang* and *FUEL* both occur in the colligation *V n*, where semantic conformity can be discovered. *FUEL* habitually co-occurs with a bundle of one-off nouns, including *hatreds*, *hate*, *anger*, *annoyance*, *anti-German feeling*, *psychological addiction*, and *nationalism*. These lexical choices all point to a semantic preference of 'strong unpleasant emotions or mentality'. To the right of 助长 *zhuzhang*, the semantic preference of 'tendency/habit' is evident, which can be (i) a social tendency prevailing among a group of people, or (ii) a mental tendency of an individual or group. The recurrent collocates for the two semantic sets include:

(i) Social tendency
  发展 *fazhan* (development), 之风 *zhifeng* (tendency), 风气 *fengqi* (habit), 风 *feng* (a suffix that must be attached to a noun to denote a habit), 倾向 *qingxiang* (tendency)
(ii) Mental tendency
  不满和气愤 *buman he qifen* (discontent and anger), 主义 *zhuyi* (-ism), 思想 *sixiang* (ideology), 心理 *xinli* (mentality)

Nouns in group (ii) and the aforesaid noun collocates of *FUEL* have common semantic features of 'emotion' or 'mentality'. This indicates that the two verbs are likely to exhibit similar semantic expectations. It is also found that some noun collocates of 助长 *zhuzhang* show a strong reliance on pre-noun modifiers to specify the negative mentality. Examples of the modifier-noun co-occurrences (pre-noun modifiers are in bold) are:

Example (4)

个人主义 *geren zhuyi* (**individualism**)

Example (5)

腐化思想 *fuhua sixiang* (**corrupt** thought)

Example (6)

依赖心理 *yilai xinli* (**dependent** mentality)

Example (7)

官僚主义 *guanliao zhuyi* (**bureaucratism**)

Example (8)

唯利是图的思想 *weilishitu de sixiang* (**mercenary** thought)

助长 *zhuzhang* is occasionally accompanied by amplifiers in its left co-text, such as 更 *geng* (more) and 更加 *gengjia* (to a higher degree), which reinforce the seriousness of a tendency or consequence. At the same position, negative expressions—including 不会 *buhui* (cannot), 决不会 *juebuhui* (absolutely cannot), and 决不可以 *juebukeyi* (never can)—are also detected to deny the act of 助长 *zhuzhang*. By comparison, these optional preferences are rare to the left of *FUEL*.

In spite of the differences in collocational behaviour or optional preference, when co-occurring with the obligatory preference 'emotion or mentality', the two verbs both convey a central meaning of 'to increase the strength or degree of something undesirable'. This means that the semantic correspondence between 助长 *zhuzhang* and *FUEL* is achieved in company with similar semantic preferences.

Unsurprisingly, the co-occurrence of the two verbs with 'unpleasant emotions or mentality' generally contributes to a negative semantic prosody. In universal terms, no one expects the increase of undesirable emotions; instead, we normally consider these undesirabilities as something serious and may seek to root them out. In this sense, the negative prosody of 'severity' is easy to identify. With the same prosodic norm, the following pattern equivalence is strongly suggested.

Pattern Equivalence 1

([amplification/negation]$_{PREF}$) 助长 ***zhuzhang*** [unpleasant mental tendency]$_{PREF}$
⟹ [severity]$_{PROS}$ Neg. PSI = 0.8
FUEL [strong unpleasant emotion/mentality]$_{PREF}$
⟹ [severity]$_{PROS}$ Neg. PSI = 0.67

In terms of prosodic strength, the negative PSI attached to 助长 *zhuzhang* is 0.8, while that for *FUEL* is 0.67. The above pattern equivalence means that when 助长 *zhuzhang* co-occurs with 'mental tendency', which is negative in meaning, and *FUEL* co-occurs with 'strong undesirable emotions', the resultant patterns both inevitably deliver a negative attitudinal meaning.

FUEL and 助长 *zhuzhang* also display similarities in semantic preference and prosody in another lexicogrammatical environment. *FUEL* shows a strong collocation with nouns expressing a 'financial or social phenomenon'. It is found that a majority of collocates are straightforward in denoting 'financial or social issues', including *inflation* ($f = 5$), *growth* ($f = 2$), *uncertainty* ($f = 2$), *unemployment*, *debts*, *market for fakes and forgeries*, *decline*, *poaching*, and *drugs trade*. To the left of these nouns, there is an occasional collocation with attributive adjectives such as *fiery*, *unsustainable*, *widespread*, and *massive*, which indicate that the situation is spreading, deteriorating, and uncontrollable. Thus, the semantic prosody can be identified as 'severity and harshness', with a negative PSI of 0.63.

助长 *zhuzhang* also tends to co-occur with the semantic preference of 'social phenomenon or activities', which is realized by expressions such as 投机活动 *touji huodong* (profiteering activities), 盲目生产 *mangmu shengchan* (blind production), and 重复建设 *chongfu jianshe* (duplicated construction). The negative atmosphere is often reinforced by pre-node expressions, including 或者 *huozhe* (or), 往往 *wangwang* (often), and 足以 *zuyi* (it is enough to), which indicate the probable results of the action. Again, the semantic prosody could be termed 'severity', with a negative PSI of 0.62.

Despite colligational differences and collocational diversities, the two verbs are matched at the level of semantic preference and semantic prosody. Pattern equivalence, as shown below, can be proposed for a similar semantic preference of 'social phenomenon', the same semantic prosody of 'severity', and closer semantic prosody strengths, with 0.62 for 助长 *zhuzhang* and 0.63 for *FUEL*.

Pattern Equivalence 2

([possibility]$_{\text{PREF}}$) **助长 *zhuzhang*** [social phenomenon or activities]$_{\text{PREF}}$
⟹ [severity]$_{\text{PROS}}$ Neg. PSI = 0.62
FUEL [financial or social phenomenon]$_{\text{PREF}}$
⟹ [severity]$_{\text{PROS}}$ Neg. PSI = 0.63

3.3 平息 *pingxi* Versus *ASSUAGE*

In this section, we are committed to the analysis of 平息 *pingxi* and *ASSUAGE*, focusing on correspondences in terms of semantic preference and semantic prosody.

3.3.1 Co-selection Patterns of 平息 *pingxi* and *ASSUAGE*

A scrutiny of 87 hits of 平息 *pingxi* in the MCC shows that the verb is involved in four patterns of co-selection, presented in Table 6.

As shown above, 平息 *pingxi* invariably co-occurs with object nouns having the semantic feature of 'disturbance' but, in each pattern, this inherent semantic preference gets realized in different sets of words of specific meanings. Furthermore, 平息 *pingxi* is occasionally preceded by negatives, modals, or adverbs that point to optional semantic preferences distinctive in form and meaning in different patterns.

It is noted that 平息 *pingxi* consistently conveys a positive semantic prosody, with high indexes of PS in all the patterns. Pattern 1 constitutes the major pattern of 平息 *pingxi*, making up 36% of all the instances.

Table 6 Patterns and PSI associated with 平息 *pingxi*

Patterns	PSI
Pattern 1 (36%) ([by force]$_{PREF}$) 平息 *pingxi* [riot/rebellion against the government]$_{PREF}$ ([devotion]$_{PREF}$) $\Longrightarrow$ [paying great cost to quell riots]$_{PROS}$	Pos. 1.0
Pattern 2 (35%) ([difficulty]$_{PREF}$) 平息 *pingxi* [trouble/dispute causing agitation]$_{PREF}$ $\Longrightarrow$ [making efforts to calm down a disturbing matter]$_{PROS}$	Pos. 0.81
Pattern 3 (20%) ([difficulty]$_{PREF}$) 平息 *pingxi* [mental state of emotional disturbance]$_{PREF}$ $\Longrightarrow$ [struggling with strong and disturbing emotions]$_{PROS}$	Pos. 0.88
Pattern 4 (9%) ([gradualness]$_{PREF}$) 平息 *pingxi* [disturbing sounds or things]$_{PREF}$ $\Longrightarrow$ [expecting disturbing noises to subside]$_{PROS}$	Pos. 1.0

Table 7 Patterns and PSI associated with *ASSUAGE*

Patterns	PSI
Pattern 1 (67%) ([difficulty]$_{PREF}$) *ASSUAGE* [strong and unpleasant emotion]$_{PREF}$ $\Longrightarrow$ [struggling with overwhelming emotions]$_{PROS}$	Pos. 0.88
Pattern 2 (22%) ([difficulty]$_{PREF}$) *ASSUAGE* [troubles/problematic situations]$_{PREF}$ $\Longrightarrow$ [trying to mitigate something unpleasant and serious]$_{PROS}$	Pos. 0.86
Pattern 3 (11%) *ASSUAGE* [desire/need]$_{PREF}$ $\Longrightarrow$ [willing satisfy needs]$_{PROS}$	Pos. 0.82

The word *ASSUAGE*, on the other hand, is found to be embedded in the three patterns presented in Table 7.

As Table 7 shows, the nouns or noun phrases as objects of the verb fall into three semantic sets: 'strong and unpleasant emotion/feeling', 'troubles/problematic situations', and 'desire/need'. The semantic preference of 'difficulty' occasionally emerges to the left of *ASSUAGE* and is mainly realized by negatives, modals, or adverbs. The concordances below show the optional semantic preference of 'difficulty', with its lexical realizations underlined:

Example (9)

...cussed it with him. My apologies did little to **assuage** the situation and I was informed that...

Example (10)

...eing, a dull, aching pain that could never be **assuaged**. She walked into the flat, and...

Example (11)

...er: the memory of whose dying he could not **assuage**: Bearing gifts of flowers and sweet nuts...

Example (12)

...their feelings. Party opinions were partially **assuaged** by a protest meeting at the Carlton Clu...

Example (13)

...nd those pangs which had been temporarily **assuaged** by what it had found in the wall...

The semantic prosody can be perceived as positive for all three patterns associated with *ASSUAGE*, which expresses the meaning of exerting efforts to mitigate something unpleasant and serious. Pattern 1, comprising 67% of all the concordances studied, is the major pattern of *ASSUAGE*.

3.3.2 Pattern Equivalence Between 平息 *pingxi* and *ASSUAGE*

In their respective contexts, both verbs tend to co-occur with the semantic preference 'mood/emotion', and we confine the following discussion to the collocational profiles constituting this preference and cross-language equivalence. *ASSUAGE* is found to collocate strongly with words expressing a strong emotion or mental state.

Recurrent collocates include *fears*, *guilt*, *loneliness*, *misery*, *anxieties*, *concern*, and *pride*. This preference occurs with a high frequency to the right of the node verb and, occasionally, to its left in the passive voice. Immediately to the left of the node, there is a noticeable semantic preference for 'difficulty', which is often realized by negatives or semi-modals of tentativeness:

> Negatives: *not really*, *evidently not*, *was not*, *did not*, *did little to*, *could not*
> Semi-modals: *aimed at*, *trying to*, *aimed to*, *in an effort to*

ASSUAGE co-selecting the preferences of 'strong mood/emotion' and 'difficulty' delivers the meaning that one is having difficulty trying to lessen overwhelming emotions. The semantic prosody can be postulated as generally favourable because it is always desirable to make an unpleasant feeling less severe. The co-selections between the node verb, semantic preferences, and prosody give rise to the major pattern of *ASSUAGE*, which accounts for 60% of the 100 instances and shows a PSI of 0.88.

A scrutiny of the concordances of 平息 *pingxi* shows that a group of noun collocates belong to the semantic set of 'strong emotion/mental state'. This preference is realized by a bundle of one-off nouns, including 怨恨 *yuanhen* (resentment), 不满 *buman* (discontent), 不安 *buan* (unease), 怒气 *nuqi* (anger), and 心潮 *xinchao* (a surge of emotions). Moreover, a set of *adj n* combinations accentuates the extent of the 'strong mental state':

Example (14)

激动的情感 *jidong de qinggan* (excited emotions/excitement)

Example (15)

激动的感情 *jidong de ganqing* (excited emotions/excitement)

Example (16)

焦躁的心情 *jiaozao de xinqing* (anxious mood/anxiety)

Example (17)

感情的波澜 *ganqing de bolan* (emotional waves)

Example (18)

感情的万顷波涛 *ganqing de wanqingbotao* (a storm of surging emotions)

Example (19)

潮水般的思绪 *chaoshuiban de sixu* (a tidal wave of thoughts)

Another noticeable semantic feature that accompanies 平息 *pingxi* turns out to be 'difficulty', which is also the preference with which *ASSUAGE* is found to co-occur. This semantic group is mainly realized by negatives appearing on either side of the node; for instance, 没有平息 *meiyou pingxi* (not assuage), 再也无法平息 *zaiye wuf pingxi* (can no longer assuage), 平息不下来 *pingxi buxialai* (cannot assuage), and 平息不了 *pingxi buliao* (cannot assuage) (negatives in Chinese and English are underlined).

The preference of 'difficulty' is also reinforced by pre-node adverbs, including 理智地 *lizhide* (sensibly), 久久 *jiujiu* (for a long time), and 渐次 *jianci* (gradually). The information of co-selection leads to the Pattern 3 of 平息 *pingxi*. This pattern of co-selection conveys the meaning that one is trying in vain to lessen or restrain a strong and disturbing emotion. In a general sense, efforts made to overcome an overwhelming emotion are considered sensible and, sometimes, desirable. Therefore, this pattern is associated with a favourable prosody and the PSI is 0.88.

Taking account of the semantic preference and prosody, we can now establish the pattern equivalence between 平息 *pingxi* and *ASSUAGE* as follows:

Pattern Equivalence

([difficulty]$_{\text{PREF}}$) **平息** ***pingxi*** [mental state of emotional disturbance]$_{\text{PREF}}$

$\Longrightarrow$ [struggling with strong and disturbing emotions]$_{\text{PROS}}$ Pos. PSI = 0.88

([difficulty]$_{PREF}$) ***ASSUAGE*** [strong and unpleasant emotion]$_{PREF}$ $\Longrightarrow$ [struggling with overwhelming emotions]$_{PROS}$ Pos. PSI = 0.88.

4 Discussion of Pattern Equivalence

In this section, we have identified patterns and established pattern equivalence in contrastive linguistic contexts. The phraseologies of words in contrastive linguistic contexts show great variances. A word under scrutiny is likely to be associated with more than one pattern, and its major pattern does not necessarily correspond to the major pattern of its counterpart in another language.

At the level of collocation, either party of a presumed translation pair can exhibit a wide range of collocational choices. However, semantic resemblance between a translation pair does not exist because of the overlaps of collocates but, rather, because of the fact that a word 'demands not a specific word but a semantically defined class of words' (Bublitz 1998: 25). In other words, the diversified lexical choices can be classified into groups based on the semantic consistency they share. For this reason, the scope of translation units should be enlarged from single words to EUMs by incorporating comparisons of semantic preferences in a translation pair.

The patterns we have arrived at indicate that semantic preference is the level at which similarities are more common than distinctions. Although there is always a diversity of lexical realizations right down to actual words, all the choices point to certain semantic preferences. It is noted that to propose pattern equivalence there must be at least more than one inherent or necessary semantic preference in common. Differences in an occasional or optional semantic preference could not have a definite impact on pattern equivalence. For instance, in combination with the inherent semantic preference 'power', 夺取 *duoqu*, can be preceded by an optional preference 'men of a social class', while *SEIZE* can be accompanied optionally by words of 'intention'. This difference in meaning, however, does not affect their conformity in semantic prosody.

At the level of semantic prosody, pattern equivalence can be recognized by assessing the respective prosodic norm and PSI of each presumed pair. High indexes of agreeing prosodies suggest a high probability of pattern equivalence. For instance, 平息 *pingxi* and *ASSUAGE* display remarkable semantic resemblance in the co-occurrence with an inherent preference, 'unpleasant emotion', and an optional preference, 'difficulty'. Moreover, both patterns have the same positive PSI of 0.88 and, in this case, pattern equivalence is strongly indicated. It is interesting to note that there are patterns that do not show an invariably positive or negative prosody. The next section discusses how a divergent prosody or an altered component in a pattern can affect the assessment of pattern equivalence.

5 Pattern Equivalence and Meaning-Shift Units

In exploring local grammar, Sinclair (2010: 44) proposes the notion of meaning-shift, regarding which he claims that 'each of the lexical components of the lexical item should show a meaning-shift from its use outside the lexical item'. In Sinclair's terms, 'lexical item', here, means a unit of meaning that results from local grammar; that is, lexicogrammatical co-selection, which in this study is referred to as 'pattern'. This claim highlights that, once a unit of meaning is identified, each lexical component has its meaning settled, and that the meaning of a lexical component should change when it occurs in a different unit of meaning. In this section, we examine, in the contrastive linguistic context, how the shift of one component within a pattern could affect pattern equivalence.

5.1 Shift of Semantic Prosody

According to Sinclair (1996), semantic prosody is the most abstract and obligatory component of an EUM. Our analysis in the previous section shows that there are instances that run counter to the prosodic norm of a pattern. In light of this, it is worthwhile discussing the nature of counter-examples for cross-language equivalence.

As shown above, when 夺取 *duoqu* and *SEIZE* show a semantic preference of 'place' and are associated with a negative semantic prosody, they can be viewed as equivalents. But 23% of cases for the pattern 夺取 *duoqu* also deliver a positive prosody. Seven counter-examples are detected in the MCC, one of which is presented as Example (20).

Example (20)

我们终于打败日本侵略者，**夺取**了全中国。

We finally defeated the Japanese invaders, and ***seized*** the whole of China.

In Example (20), 夺取 *duoqu* co-occurring with 全中国 *quanzhongguo* (the whole of China) suggests few clues as to the semantic prosody. The reading of the underlying attitudinal meaning relies greatly on the co-text. In Example (20), the subject *we* refers to the Chinese people who fought against the Japanese invaders during World War II.

It is obvious that the writer of Example (20) is attempting to deliver a positive attitude toward this historical event. In translation practice, the original communicative purpose in the source language has to be maintained. *SEIZE* is not the appropriate word for translating 夺取 *duoqu*, because, occurring in the same semantic environment, *SEIZE* generates an overwhelmingly negative semantic prosody in the target language. In other words, the shift of semantic prosody in the original language does not match the default prosody in the target language. In the present case, *took over* can be a better translation equivalent.

Our analysis indicates that instances of semantic prosody shifting from one polarity to the other are not uses of irony, which depend on a clash with a sufficiently expected background of collocation norms (Louw 1993). In fact, the change in semantic prosody often gives rise to a meaning-shift unit (Sinclair 2010), and the translation equivalence is liable to change. Unawareness of a shift from the prosodic norm could have the original attitudinal meaning distorted in the target language.

As a further illustration, let us turn to other instances of shifts from the prosodic norm identified in patterns associated with 助长 *zhuzhang* and *FUEL*. The pattern equivalence between them is repeated below.

([possibility]$_{\mathrm{PREF}}$) 助长 *zhuzhang* [social phenomenon or activities]$_{\mathrm{PREF}}$
$\Longrightarrow$ [severity]$_{\mathrm{PROS}}$ Neg. PSI = 0.62
FUEL [financial or social phenomenon]$_{\mathrm{PREF}}$
$\Longrightarrow$ [severity]$_{\mathrm{PROS}}$ Neg. PSI = 0.63

FUEL, apart from its habitual co-selection with the semantic preference 'financial or social issues', also co-occurs, as previously noted, with words expressing a 'desirable social phenomenon'; for instance, *economic growth*, *massive development*, *city boom*, and *consumption*, and *the growth in health insurance*. These co-occurring expressions tend to deliver and reinforce a positive semantic prosody of a 'promising outlook', which seems to diverge from the negative prosodic norm.

In this sense, *FUEL* is involved in a pattern that is composed of the core, a semantic preference of 'desirable social phenomenon', and a semantic prosody of 'promising outlook'. This pattern, though used infrequently, distinguishes itself from the major pattern, which consists of the core, a semantic preference of a 'social or financial issue,' and a negative prosody of 'severity'.

Apparently, the shift of semantic prosody constructs another unit of meaning, rather than the exploitation of semantic prosody for rhetorical effect. The reversed semantic prosody is incongruous with the negative prosodic norm inherent in the major pattern of 助长 *zhuzhang*. In this case, 促进 *cujin* (contribute to) may be a better translation than 助长 *zhuzhang*, because 促进 *cujin* has a higher probability of conveying positive attitudinal meaning in Chinese. Evidence suggests that counter-examples to the prosodic norm are likely to constitute a meaning-shift unit (Sinclair 2010), that is, a new pattern of co-selection which, in turn, requires different pattern equivalence.

In a similar vein, the co-occurrences of 助长 *zhuzhang* with words indicating 'growth' conspicuously run counter to its negative prosodic norm. We encountered a few instances of 助长 *zhuzhang* co-occurring with words expressing 'desirable growth':

助长 *zhuzhang* 知识发展 *zhishi fazhan* 'the growth of knowledge'
生产力发展 *shengchanli fazhan* 'the development of productivity'
农产物的增加改良 *nongchanwu de zengjiagailiang* 'improvement of agricultural products'

The above instances from the MCC are not typical uses and they are opposite to the normal expectations of Chinese native speakers for the collocational behaviour of the word in question. In this particular context, it seems that the negative prosody associated with the verb is bleached out by the collocates 发展 *fazhan* (development) and 改良 *gailiang* (improvement). Therefore, the phraseological unit has the overall function of delivering a favourable attitude towards a desirable growth.

As a result we encounter a very infrequent pattern that comprises a positive semantic prosody, a semantic preference of 'desirable growth', and the core. This minor pattern deviates from the above pattern of 助长 *zhuzhang* in semantic prosody and semantic preference. It indicates that the shift of semantic prosody leads to a new pattern of co-selection, though the pattern may be an infrequent or idiosyncratic use. In this case, *FUEL* cannot be an acceptable equivalent, as the in-built negative semantic prosody may well generate an unfavourable attitude in English texts.

In sum, the analysis of counter-examples reveals that divergence from the prosodic norm is not necessarily for ironic or stylistic effects; rather, it may well be an idiosyncratic use, or constitute a meaning-shift unit that is realized in an infrequent co-selection pattern. This divergence from a normal prosody associated with a pattern can be explained by the lexical priming theory of Hoey (2005). As Morley and Partington (2009: 146) argue, this means that the 'normal priming prosodies can always be switched off or overridden or exploited by users'.

Analysis shows that an overturned semantic prosody undoubtedly leads to the change of translation equivalence. When native speakers of a language are strongly primed to associate a pattern with a particular prosody, the deviation from the prosodic norm in the source language texts could be infrequent or untypical uses. To render the meaning properly into the target language requires a different lexical pattern, or the attitudinal meaning would be misinterpreted.

5.2 Specificity of Collocational Choice

In Sect. 3.3.2, pattern equivalence taking 平息 *pingxi* and *ASSUAGE* as cores was proposed. However, we note that, although *ASSUAGE* collocates with words denoting unpleasant emotion, not all of the collocates from this semantic set can be perfectly matched with those co-occurring with 平息 *pingxi*. Table 8 illustrates the collocational profiles of the two words in question.

As shown in Table 8, the collocates of 平息 *pingxi* and *ASSUAGE* display a partial correspondence. It is noticeable that the well-matched collocates of the two verbs in group (i) have similar semantic features: 'intense', 'suffering', and 'overwhelming'. In contrast, non-corresponding collocates in group (ii) may disrupt correspondence and equivalence.

Whereas collocates of 平息 *pingxi* in group (ii) accentuate the moods or emotions that are disturbing, uncontrollable, and surging like turbulent waves, collocates of *ASSUAGE* in group (ii) seem to denote less violent or fierce emotions. Since the second group of collocates of the two verbs differs in terms of specific semantic features,

Table 8 Collocational correspondence between 平息 *pingxi* versus *ASSUAGE*

Translatability	Collocates of *ASSUAGE*	Collocates of 平息 *pingxi*
ASSUAGE = 平息 *pingxi*	(i) *fears, anxieties, discontent, anger*	(i) 怨恨 *yuanhen* (resentment), 不满 *buman* (discontent), 不安 *buan* (unease), 怒气 *nuqi* (anger), 焦躁的心情 *jiaozao de xinqing* (anxious mood/anxiety)
ASSUAGE ≠ 平息 *pingxi*	(ii) *guilt, loneliness, misery, concern, pride, doubts, grief, conscience*	(ii) 心潮 *xinchao* (a surge of emotions), 激动的情感 *jidong de qinggan* (excited emotions/excitement) 激动的感情 *jidong de ganqing* (excited emotions/excitement) 感情的波澜 *ganqing de bolan* (emotional waves) 感情的万顷波涛 *ganqing de wanqingbotao* (a storm of surging emotions) 潮水般的思绪 *chaoshuiban de sixu* (a tidal wave of thoughts)

semantic correspondence cannot be fulfilled appropriately in these lexical circumstances.

The non-correspondence at the collocational level is due to the fact that 平息 *pingxi* strongly predicts the semantic feature 'emotional torment' and 'inner struggle', so the lexical choices are restricted to this expectation. In bilingual contexts, if the collocates of *ASSUAGE* do not have such semantic features, pattern equivalence cannot be proposed satisfactorily.

In view of this finding, we reassessed 平息 *pingxi* and *ASSUAGE* in the SJTU Parallel Corpus, and found one problematic instance, shown below with the node in bold and the noun collocate underlined:

与此密切相关的概念是"和平发展"运动,以 **平息** 外国对中国的军事现代化及其全球化的<u>评议</u>
is the 'peaceful development' campaign to **assuage** foreign <u>concerns</u> over China's military

The collocation *assuage concerns* seems odd for 平息评议 *pingxi pingyi*, because the collocates, *concerns* and 评议 *pingyi*, seem to express different meanings. While 评议 *pingyi* generally indicates remarks and criticisms, *concerns* refers to the attention paid to something one thinks important. In the Chinese instance, 评议 *pingyi* implies offensive criticisms for interfering in the internal affairs of one's country. In this case, *assuage criticism* is suggested as a better translation, and this collocation is also found in instances from the BNC.

To sum up, 平息 *pingxi* and *ASSUAGE* can be established as equivalents in their respective patterns; however, exactly identical semantic preferences are impossible. Even though a translation pair demonstrates a similar semantic preference, the collocates realizing the preference cannot be well-matched. It is noted that parts of the collocates are matched, but habitual collocates of a word may not be equally expected by its equivalents in another language. This result is in line with Kübler and Volanschi's (2012) argument that, although the English word *COMMIT* and its French counterpart *COMMETTRE* are associated with the same semantic prosody, they have different collocational profiles that should be listed for translation.

The collocational non-correspondence between 平息 *pingxi* and *ASSUAGE* lies in the fact that, under the same umbrella of 'strong mood/emotion', the Chinese verb 平息 *pingxi* requires the specificity of this preference; that is, the lexical choices are restricted to 'intense and disturbing emotions'. This collocational restriction demands that collocates of its English counterparts should have the same specificity in meaning. If a collocate goes beyond the range of semantic features expected by the node, correspondence at the collocational level will show a complex picture.

It should be noted that, with the semantic preference unchanged, the shift of collocational choice cannot affect semantic prosody and the recognized pattern. Pattern equivalence cannot be overturned as well, though collocational correspondence may seem to be awkward and infrequent. In a word, particular collocations that defy generalized semantic preferences and semantic prosodies disturb cross-language equivalence, but only to a certain extent.

6 Conclusion

This study set out to investigate the complex relationships between patterns of co-selection and cross-language equivalence. Drawing on the framework of EUMs (Sinclair 1996), the features of collocation, semantic preference, and semantic prosody of three translation pairs extracted from a bi-directional Chinese–English parallel corpus were examined.

By way of a contrastive analysis, different co-selection patterns of translation pairs were identified. Complex relationships between semantic prosody, semantic preference, collocation, and cross-language equivalence have been explored through the examination of the two comparable corpora.

Contrastive linguistic evidence indicates that semantic prosody plays a crucial role for achieving and maintaining cross-language equivalence in presumed translation pairs. First, semantic prosody is inherently associated with a phraseological pattern of a word, to the extent that the change of a prosodic meaning from the favourable to the unfavourable, or vice versa, is bound to alter cross-language equivalence fundamentally. In general terms, a shift in semantic prosody results from a change in the co-selection pattern. In other words, it is the change of pattern, rather than the change of a single word, that brings about the change of meaning. This is arguably an important motif and shows why John Sinclair (2010) renamed the original 'lexical item' as 'the meaning-shift unit'.

Second, prosodic strength, as a practical means by to indicate the polarity of semantic prosody, is a useful reference criterion for establishing cross-language equivalence. A high prosodic strength reveals the prosodic norm associated with a pattern in the source language text, and can offer translators insights for choosing appropriate word patterns in the target language text. In the case of the divergence of semantic prosody, the aim is not necessarily the exploitation of a prosodic norm for rhetorical effect but may, rather, express a different but genuine meaning with a varied co-selection pattern. In translation, divergence from the prosodic norm of a word in the target language may misrender the original attitudinal meaning which, again, calls attention to the important role of semantic prosody, and to the fact that an appropriate choice of co-selection patterns is of utmost importance for translators.

The study has also found that there is a complex inter-relationship between collocation, semantic preference, semantic prosody, and cross-language equivalence. On the whole, well-matched or identical collocations and semantic preferences are rare for the translation pairs under study, and it is the interaction of the five categories of co-selection that brings about an attitudinal meaning.

Correspondence in terms of inherent semantic preference is obligatory in establishing pattern equivalence because the inherent semantic preference delivers the primary message of a pattern and navigates the direction of attitudinal meaning. Some optional preferences, emerging either occasionally or farther away from the node, show low probability of co-selection with the node. Though it helps to reinforce a prevailing prosody, optional preference seems to be less important in assessing pattern equivalence. At the collocation level, a wide variety of variations may pop up for translation pairs under study. However, each preference exerts restrictions on the lexical choices. It is therefore a good strategy to ensure specificity of collocational choices within practicable categories of semantic preference, which can, for the most part, lead to a discovery of similarities and differences in usage patterns.

This study can have practical implications for corpus-based contrastive linguistic and translation studies, and foreign-language teaching. The study has offered a clear indication that word-level candidates for translation equivalents may not help render meanings appropriately in translation and could result in the phenomenon of 'false friends' (Partington 1998) when semantic prosody is considered. It is suggested that a proper awareness of the roles of semantic preference and prosody could help translators and translation researchers understand the nature of equivalence more properly. It is also fairly evident that, if greater weight is given to the co-selection patterns of words, this will help improve the performance of foreign-language learners and translators.

This study is intended as a synchronic description of cross-language equivalence of co-selection. There is also plenty of research potential regarding equivalence through the diachronic lens. It will also be interesting to explore genre specific or domain specific prosodies and meaning-shift units across languages, particularly between English and Chinese.

References

Altenberg, B. (1999). Adverbial Connectors in English and Swedish: Semantic and Lexical Correspondences. In H. Hasselgård & S. Oksefjell (Eds.), *Out of Corpora: Studies in Honour of Stig Johansson* (pp. 249–268). Amsterdam: Rodopi.

Bednarek, M. (2008). Semantic Preference and Semantic Prosody Re-examined. *Corpus Linguistics and Linguistic Theory, 4*(2), 119–139.

Berber-Sardinha, T. (2000). Semantic Prosodies in English and Portuguese: A Contrastive Study. *Cuadernos de Filologia Inglesa, 9*(1), 93–110.

Bublitz, W. (1998). 'I Entirely Dot Dot Dot': Copying Semantic Features in Collocations with Up-Scaling Intensifiers. In S. Rainer (Ed.), *Making Meaningful Choices in English* (pp. 11–32). Tübingen: Narr.

Dam-Jensen, H., & Zethsen, K. K. (2007). Pragmatic Patterns and the Lexical System: A Reassessment of Evaluation in Language. *Journal of Pragmatics, 39*(9), 1608–1623.

Hoey, M. (2005). *Lexical Priming: A New Theory of Words and Language*. London and New York: Routledge.

Hunston, S. (2002). *Corpora in Applied Linguistics*. Cambridge: Cambridge University Press.

Hunston, S. (2007). Semantic Prosody Revisited. *International Journal of Corpus Linguistics, 12*(2), 249–268.

Kübler, N., & Volanschi, A. (2012). Semantic Prosody and Specialised Translation, or How a Lexico-Grammatical Theory of Language Can Help with Specialized Translation. In A. Boulton, S. Carter-Thomas, & E. Rowley-Jolivet (Eds.), *Corpus-Informed Research and Learning in ESP: Issues and Applications* (pp. 105–135). Amsterdam: John Benjamins.

Louw, B. (1993). Irony in the Text or Insincerity in the Writer? The Diagnostic Potential of Semantic Prosodies. In M. Baker, G. Francis, & E. Tognini-Bonelli (Eds.), *Text and Technology: In Honour of John Sinclair* (pp. 157–176). Amsterdam: John Benjamins.

Morley, J., & Partington, A. (2009). A Few Frequently Asked Questions About Semantic—Or Evaluative—Prosody. *International Journal of Corpus Linguistics, 14*(2), 139–158.

Nelson, M. (2006). Semantic Associations in Business English: A Corpus-Based Analysis. *International Journal of Corpus Linguistics, 11*(4), 513–514.

Partington, A. (1998). *Patterns and Meanings: Using Corpora for English Language Research and Teaching*. Amsterdam: John Benjamins.

Partington, A. (2004). 'Utterly Content in Each Other's Company': Some Thoughts on Semantic Prosody and Semantic Preference. *International Journal of Corpus Linguistics, 9*(1), 131–156.

Sinclair, J. (1991). *Corpus Concordance Collocation*. Oxford: Oxford University Press.

Sinclair, J. (1996). The Search for Units of Meaning. *TEXTUS: English Studies in Italy, 9*(1), 75–106.

Sinclair, J. (2004). *Trust the Text*. London: Routledge.

Sinclair, J. (2010). Defining the Definiendum. In G.-M. de Schryver (Ed.), *A Way with Words: Recent Advances in Lexical Theory and Analysis* (pp. 37–47). Uganda: Menha Publishers.

Stewart, D. (2009). Safeguarding the Lexicogrammatical Environment: Translating Semantic Prosody. In B. Allison, P. R. Inés, & P. S. Gijón (Eds.), *Corpus Use and Translating: Corpus Use for Learning to Translate and Learning Corpus Use to Translate* (pp. 29–46). Amsterdam and Philadelphia: John Benjamins.

Stewart, D. (2010). *Semantic Prosody: A Critical Evaluation*. New York: Routledge.

Stubbs, M. (1995). Collocations and Semantic Profiles: On the Cause of the Trouble with Quantitative Studies. *Functions of Language, 2*(1), 23–55.

Stubbs, M. (2001). *Words and Phrases*. Oxford and Malden: Blackwell.

Tognini-Bonelli, E. (2002). Functionally Complete Units of Meaning Across English and Italian: Towards a Corpus-Driven Approach. In B. Altenberg & S. Granger (Eds.), *Lexis in Contrast: Corpus-Based Approaches* (pp. 73–95). Amsterdam: John Benjamins.

Wei, N. (2011). Corpus-Based Contrastive Studies of Phraseology. *Foreign Languages, 34*(4), 32–42.

Wei, N., & Li, X. (2014). Exploring Semantic Preference and Semantic Prosody Across English and Chinese: Their Roles for Cross-Linguistic Equivalence. *Corpus Linguistics and Linguistic Theory, 10*(1), 103–138.

Xiao, R. (2010). How Different Is Translated Chinese from Native Chinese? *International Journal of Corpus Linguistics, 15*(1), 5–35.

Xiao, R., & McEnery, T. (2006). Collocation, Semantic Prosody and Near Synonymy: A Cross-Linguistic Perspective. *Applied Linguistics, 27*(1), 103–129.

Looking for Translators' Fingerprints: A Corpus-based Study on Chinese Translations of *Ulysses*

Qing Wang and Defeng Li

1 Introduction

In highlighting the importance of style in literary translation, Boase-Beier maintains that style exerts its effects upon translation in at least three ways:

> Firstly, in the actual process of translation, the way the style of the source text is viewed will affect the translator's reading of the text. Secondly, because the re-creative process in the target text will also be influenced by the sorts of choices the translator makes, and style is the outcome of choice (as opposed to those aspects of language which are not open to

This article was originally published in *Literary Linguistic Computing, 27*(1), 81–93.

Q. Wang
Shandong Jiaotong University, Jinan, China

D. Li (✉)
University of Macau, Macau SAR, China
e-mail: defengli@um.edu.mo

K. Hu and K. H. Kim (eds.), *Corpus-based Translation and Interpreting Studies in Chinese Contexts*, Palgrave Studies in Translating and Interpreting,
https://doi.org/10.1007/978-3-030-21440-1_6

> option), the translator's own style will become part of the target text. And, thirdly, the sense of what style is will affect not only what the translator does but how the critic of translation interprets what the translator has done. (Boase-Beier 2006: 1)

Boase-Beier's remarks—that 'the translator's own style will become part of the target text'—set us thinking on two planes: (a) a translator's choice constitutes a style of their own; and (b) the style of the target text is the outcome of both the author *and* the translator. As a text producer, the author or the translator builds their style through choices of words and structures, similar to an architect cultivating their style of building with bricks and patterns according to their taste and purpose. Boase-Beier's remark is insightful, for she distinctly articulates that the translator inevitably leaves their stylistic trait in the translation. In the target text, there is the translator's visible presence in the words they favour, the structures they prefer, and the rhetoric they like. No matter how much the translator desires to reproduce the authorial style, they will inevitably leave traces of their own style in the translation. Baker (2000) compares these traces to translators' 'fingerprints'. She questions the demand on the translator to reproduce exactly the style of the original, because 'it is as impossible to produce a stretch of language in a totally impersonal way as it is to handle an object without leaving one's fingerprints on it' (Baker 2000: 244).

The fingerprints metaphor reveals Baker's point of departure to be descriptive in nature. What interests her is not what a translator *should* do, but what they *do* do; she therefore approaches the translator's style from translation products already existing in the socio-cultural reality, rather than from translation theories idealized in a vacuum. Since the translator gives the source text a second life in the target socio-cultural context, the re-created being in the target context possesses features of its own. In the re-creation process, the translator's labour is felt through the selection and organization of words, the long or short sentence structures, the plain or oratorical way of speech—their fingerprints on the newly created texts.

2 Searching for Translators' Fingerprints

The problem now facing translation scholars is not 'whether individual literary translators can plausibly be assumed to use distinctive styles of their own', but 'how we might go about identifying what is distinctive about an individual translator's style' (Baker 2000: 248). Although it is evident that this identification can only be done within the framework of descriptive translation studies, it will still take scholars a long time to figure out the appropriate methodology. Baker and other pioneering scholars have carried out empirical studies on different translation products. Admitting that the empirical method 'can only be applied to strictly observable data', Toury justifies this as an appropriate method in descriptive translation studies (Toury 1995: 222, punctuation and emphasis in original):

> In fact, to my mind, the greatest contribution of experimentation lies precisely in its potential for shedding new light on the interdependencies of all factors which [may] act as constraints on translation and on the effects of these interdependencies on the process, its products, and the functions which any of them may serve in the recipient culture, and in increasing their predictive capacity. This potential, as I see it, derives from two of the inherent traits of experimentation: relative *controllability of variables*—and high rate of *replicability*. At the same time, most of these new methods have hardly been confronted with other achievements of modern Translation Studies, with a view to increasing their relevancy to our understanding just what translation involves.

Baker (2000) initiates a comparative study to look for 'translators' fingerprints' by examining such factors as the type-token ratio, mean sentence length, and reporting structures by comparing translations by different translators—Peter Clark and Peter Bush—and finds differences between the two translators in all three aspects. However, it may not be reasonable to conclude that they are manifestations of the translators' styles because the two translators were not working on the same source texts. Therefore the differences of style reflected in the translations may be attributed to the source texts, rather than the translators' individual styles alone. Nevertheless, as a pioneering study, Baker's research is significant and the three questions she poses are worthy of consideration:

i. Is a translator's preference for specific linguistic options independent of the style of the original author?
ii. Is it independent of general preferences of the source language, and possibly the norms or poetics of a given sociolect?
iii. If the answer is yes in both cases, is it possible to explain those preferences in terms of the social, cultural, or ideological positioning of the individual translator? (Baker 2000: 248)

A comparison between the target text and source text is necessary to answer these questions. It is just for this purpose that Malmkjær creates the term *translational stylistics*, which 'takes into consideration the relationship between the translated text and its source text', asserting that 'it is not possible through stylistic analysis of a translation alone to provide a satisfactory answer to the question *why* the translation has been made to mean as it does' (Malmkjær 2004: 16). In the qualitative study on Henry William Dulcken's English translation of *The Little Match Girl*, Malmkjær studies the translator's mode of expression and choice of words as compared with those of the original author, and finds that the translator creates for the English reader a different literary universe from that created by the original author.

However, a qualitative analysis may not be as exhaustive and representative as it could be when assisted with corpus technology, as shown in some studies (Granger et al. 2007; Laviosa 2002; Mauranen 2000; Olohan 2004). One way to further the design of the studies by Baker (2000) and Malmkjær (2004) might be a comparison of diversified translations of the same text to see whether different translators demonstrate different styles in completing the same translation task. Along these lines, Marco (2004) examines different Catalan versions of Henry James's *The Turn of the Screw* and Edgar Allen Poe's *The Fall of the House of Usher*. He finds that translation often calls for a balance between the stylistic demands of the original and the norms of the receiving language and culture, and that translators sometimes bring their own stylistic priorities to their translation practice by reference to the literary movement in the history of the target language and culture (Marco 2004: 88).

Many would agree that translation involves a balance between the stylistic demands of the original and the norms of the receiving language and culture, but how do the translators strike such a balance? Can a translator's style in the target text be distinguished from the original author's style? These questions are hard to answer for, just as Bernardini (2005) acknowledges, the translator's style is likely to be superimposed on an author's style, making it very difficult to spot.

We believe that a project on translators' styles will benefit tremendously from a comparative analysis of different versions of the same source text by translators in the same linguistic and socio-cultural context. This enables the identification of stylistic features to be attributed to the human variable alone; that is, the translator, rather than anything else. It would make the best starting point for comparison if the versions were published very close in time span, so that the identified stylistic features are not possibly due to the diachronic variable of linguistic changes over time. With this in mind, we embarked on the present corpus assisted research project on the Chinese translations of *Ulysses* by James Joyce (1882–1941), who was regarded by T. S. Eliot as 'the greatest master of the English language since Milton' (Jin 2001: 225). We extended the investigation by verifying the features of Xiao's translation with those of his original Chinese writings.

3 Design of the Bilingual Corpus of *Ulysses*

There are two well-known Chinese translations of *Ulysses*, one by Qian Xiao (2005 [1994]) and the other by Di Jin (1997). Both translators brought out their finished translations of the first 12 chapters in 1994 and, in the latter half of 1994 Xiao published the rest of his translation (which was later revised in 2005). Jin completed his translation of *Ulysses* in 1996 and published it in the Chinese mainland in 1997. Both translations of *Ulysses* won popularity among Chinese readers. One year after its publication, Xiao received the national prize for foreign literature awarded by the Press and Publication Bureau of the People's

Republic of China, and Jin won the same prize in 1998. It was unprecedented in the Bureau's history to award the top prizes to two different translations of the same foreign novel. The simultaneity and good quality of the two translations of *Ulysses* qualify them as ideal texts for a contrastive study.

In order to verify that a translator's style does, indeed, reflect his idiosyncratic use of the language concerned, we compared Xiao's Chinese translation of *Ulysses* with his original Chinese writings. The decision to focus on Xiao, rather than Jin, in the second part of the research was a practical one; Xiao is not only a well-versed translator, but also a prolific writer, which makes it possible for us to compare his translation with his creative writings. The short stories he wrote—such as *Silkworms* (蚕 1933), *The Captivated* (俘虏 1934), *Chestnuts* (栗子 1935), and *Sunset* (落日 1937)—were also widely read and appreciated in China. In 1938, Xiao wrote *Dreamy Valley* (梦之谷 1938), his only novel, which gained popularity among the youth for its romantic theme and lyrical diction. All these writings are collected in Xiao (2005).

However, it should be pointed out that the choice of pitting Xiao's Chinese translation of *Ulysses* against his original literary writings in the proposed style analysis can be a double-edged sword. On the one hand, as *Ulysses* is known as a stylistically unusual piece, it can fully exemplify how the issue of style, be it the author's or the translator's, has been dealt with in the (re)production process. On the other hand, it can also be argued that, as *Ulysses* has an extremely innovative style, it may necessarily be considered as a special literary piece, in which case the generalizability of the final conclusions may be indeterminate. However, as the present study is intended as a preliminary investigation, we deem it worthwhile to pursue it. Our next step would be to enlarge the corpus of Xiao's translations to include other Chinese translations he produced, in order to balance out the possible biases in the current design and, in turn (dis)confirm the conclusions of the current report.

For the purpose of the present project, a bilingual corpus of *Ulysses* (BCU) was built, as shown in Fig. 1.

The BCU consists of a parallel corpus made up of three subcorpora (the English original of *Ulysses*, Xiao's Chinese translation, and Jin's Chinese translation) and a comparable corpus made up of Xiao's

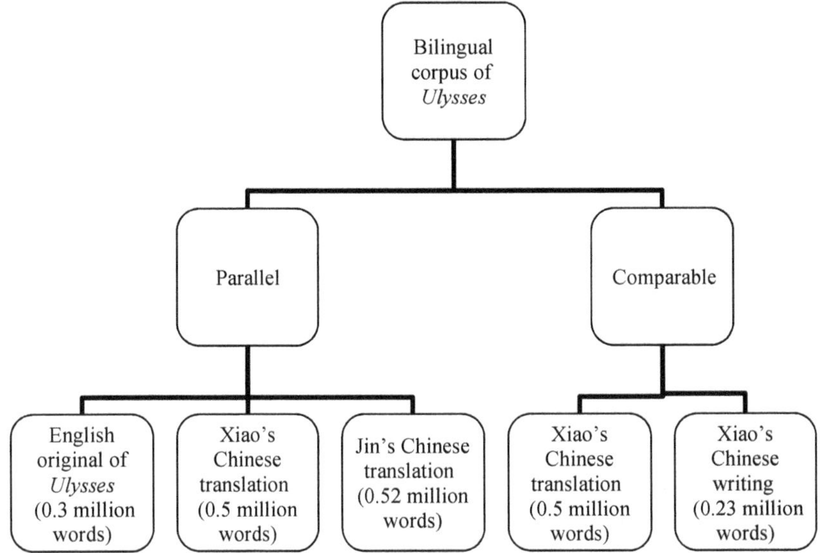

Fig. 1 Bilingual corpus of *Ulysses*

Chinese translation and his Chinese writings, including a novel and 23 short stories. The finished corpus contains over two million words. In the bilingual parallel subcorpora, the source text and the translations are aligned at the sentence level. The data retrieval software used in the study is WordSmith Tools 5.0 developed by Mike Scott.

4 Translators' Styles Manifested in Lexical Idiosyncrasy

Lexical idiosyncrasy refers to the individualized, habitual use of words. Such linguistic preference constitutes personal style. An individual's bias for a word or lexicalized expression may trigger an automatic response in his mind during the process of translation. One of the ways to probe into the translation process is through studying the translation product. The wordlist function of WordSmith Tools enables us to compare the frequency of a word in different text files. For instance, Kenny (2001) uses the wordlist function to analyse items that occur only once in her corpus to study lexical creativity in translation. Usually, the extremely high or low frequency of a word or phrase is worthy of our attention, because frequency usually reveals information about the idiosyncrasy of the text producer, and this is of special interest in our present study of translational style.

The frequency lists of two corpora can also be compared. Given two wordlists for a text and a reference corpus (RC), the WordSmith software can compare the two lists and find words that are significantly more (or less) frequent in the given text than in the RC, as is shown by the positive (or negative) statistics of keyness. In this study, the keywords of the translations by Xiao and Jin are compared because they are indicative of the translators' particular habits of language use. For that purpose, the data were all tagged for part of speech.

In order to find Xiao's idiosyncratic lexical use, the keyword list of his translation of *Ulysses* is compared with that of Jin. Table 1 shows a fraction of the results of the comparison in terms of verbs (marked v). In Table 1, the given text is Xiao's translation, and the RC is Jin's translation. Therefore, a positive keyness in Table 1 means that the word is more favoured by Xiao in his translation, whereas a negative keyness means that it is more frequently used in Jin's translation.

Differences in the preferred verbs, as illustrated in Table 1, point to a tendency to colloquialism by Xiao. While he prefers to use *xiaode* (know), a dialectal colloquial expression prevalent in Shanghai and the neighbouring areas, Jin chooses to use the standard Mandarin expression *zhidao* (know). The spoken word *qiaojian* (see) is preferred by Xiao but not by Jin, who prefers the more formal word *kan*.

Table 1 Keyword comparison of Xiao's and Jin's translations of *Ulysses*: verbs

N[a]	Key word	Freq.	%	RC Freq.	RC %	Keyness	Set
7	曉得 *xiaode* (know)	140	0.05	0		188.34	v
55	踱 *duo* (stroll)	72	0.02	5		66.98	v
70	瞧見 *qiaojian* (see)	53	0.02	2		56.97	v
266	知道 *zhidao* (know)	169	0.06	326	0.12	−57.47	v
286	看 *kan* (see)	338	0.11	647	0.23	−112.08	v

[a]*N* refers to the sequence of the words appearing in the word list

Table 2 Keyword comparison of Xiao's and Jin's translations of *Ulysses*: emotional particles

N	Key word	Freq.	%	RC Freq.	RC %	Keyness	Set
2	啦 *la*	850	0.29	165	0.06	478.65	e
9	哦 *o*	157	0.05	5		173.73	e
38	哩 *li*	172	0.06	38	0.01	87.07	e
43	喏*nuo*	95	0.03	8		82.97	e
48	嘛 *ma*	116	0.04	19		73.48	e
63	啊 *a*	431	0.15	220	0.08	61.2	e
100	噢 *o*	76	0.03	14		44.43	e
173	哎呀 *aiya*	45	0.02	8		26.98	e
264	唷 *yo*	13		79	0.03	−55.39	e

The tendency to colloquialism is also manifest in the frequency of emotional words. In spoken Chinese, the speaker's mood can find expression in tones and intonations; in the written form of the language, the writer can resort to the employment of emotional particles (e), a word class not found in English. Emotional particles can express the indicative, interrogative, imperative, and exclamatory mood of the speaker. The keyword comparison of the emotional particles in the two translations of *Ulysses* reveals that such words are used more frequently in Xiao's translation than in Jin's (Table 2).

The reason for this divergence lies in the effect Xiao aims to achieve in his translation; namely, to make the Chinese *Ulysses* 'as colloquial as possible' (Xiao 2005: 16). By using more emotional particles, the translator assigns a tone to an utterance, making it sound more emotive and familiar. In contrast, Jin resorts far less to such means, making his translation more neutral and impersonal.

Apart from the differences in formality, the stylistic variation of the two translations can also be seen in their use of lexical items. For instance, the last item in Table 1 is worth our special attention. The frequency of the use of the verb 踱 (*duo*) by the two translators presents a sharp contrast: it has 5 occurrences in Jin's translation, but 72 in Xiao's. Concordance lines generated by WordSmith Tools reveal that, in 10 instances, Xiao renders prepositions such as 'to' and 'over' into this Chinese verb and, in 62 instances, he uses it as the equivalent to 24 English verbs. Table 3 lists these English verbs and the percentage of Xiao's rendering of them

Table 3 English verbs translated into 踱 (*duo*) in Xiao's translation

Source word	Wordlist freq. (total)	Freq. of '*duo*'	%
Reapproach	1	1	100
Joggle	2	1	50.0
Trudge	4	2	50.0
Saunter	7	3	42.9
Stroll	9	3	33.3
Totter	3	1	33.3
Plod	5	1	20.0
Prowl	6	1	16.7
Shuffle	6	1	16.7
Dodge	8	1	12.5
Lurch	8	1	12.5
Turn	9	1	11.1
Stagger	13	1	7.7
Move	54	4	7.4
Walk	206	15	7.3
Creak	19	1	5.3
Proceed	21	1	4.8
Approach	30	1	3.3
Wander	32	1	3.1
Pass	198	5	2.5
Enter	46	1	2.2
Come	566	8	1.4
Go	517	6	1.2
Leave	220	1	0.5

into *duo*. According to the bilingual Contemporary Chinese Dictionary (Chinese Academy of Social Sciences 2002: 502), *duo* is defined as 慢步行走 (pace; stroll). Of all the words listed in Table 3, only *stroll* and *saunter* are often offered as the equivalents of *duo*.

In cases where Xiao repeatedly renders words such as 'walk', 'come', 'go', 'pass', and 'move' as the same word, *duo*, he actually adds a subtle nuance of meaning; that is, 'walking slowly and leisurely' to the translated text. What is more surprising is that he even renders 'dodge', 'totter', 'stagger', 'trudge', 'lurch', 'prowl', 'shuffle', and 'plod'—words referring to many different manners of walking—as the same Chinese character. As a compensatory strategy, the translator falls back on adverbial modifiers to convey the different shades of meaning in these verbs. The frequently used modifiers are 蹣跚 (*panshan*) and 踉蹌 (*liangqiang*), meaning 'unsteadily'. For example:

Example (1)

I turned around to let him have the weight of my tongue when who should I see dodging along Stony Batter only Joe Hynes. (*U* 12.3–5)
我轉過身去，剛要狠狠地罵他一頓，只見沿著斯托尼•巴特爾街蹣跚踱來的, 不是別人, 正是喬•海因斯。
Wo zhuan guo shen qu, gang yao henhen de ma ta yidun, zhijian yan zhe situoni bateer jie panshan duo lai de, bushi bieren, zhengshi qiao haiyinsi.

Example (2)

The navvy staggering forward cleaves the crowd and lurches towards the tramsiding. (*U* 15.140–141)
壯工挑著忽明忽暗的號燈, 從人叢中腳步蹣跚地踱去。
Zhuanggong tiao zhe hu ming hu an de haodeng, cong rencong zhong jiaobu panshan de duo qu.

Example (3)

Shouldering their bags they trudged, the red Egyptians. (*U* 3.370)
紅臉膛的埃及人扛著口袋, 踉踉蹌蹌踱著。
Hong liantang de aiji ren kang zhe koudai, lianglianggiangqiang duo zhe.

Example (4)

A drunken navvy ups with both hands the railings of an area, lurching heavily. (*U* 15.35–36)
一個喝得醉醺醺的壯工雙手握住地窖子前的柵欄，東倒西歪，踉踉蹌蹌地踱著。
Yige he de zuixunxun de zhuanggong shuangshou wozhu dijiaozi qian de zhalan, dongdaoxiwai, lianglianggiangqiang de duo zhe.

This brief survey of the word *duo* in the parallel corpus of *Ulysses* does seem to suggest that Xiao favoured the use of the Chinese verb *duo*. Our subsequent comparison of Xiao's Chinese writings with his Chinese translations also confirms this. We used this character as a node to search the comparable corpus and the software generated a list of 48 occurrences in Xiao's Chinese writings. We find that Xiao uses the word *duo* with a much broader sense than its conventional semantic meaning of 'stroll' as defined in the dictionary and used by many Chinese. In each of Examples (5)–(8), a literal translation is given to illustrate Xiao's preference for this character in his literary creation.

Example (5)

我疾速地來回踱著。
Wo jisu de laihui duo zhe.
I strolled rapidly to and fro.

Example (6)

那個穿黑坎肩的向遠處打了一個呼哨,一部备就的敞篷馬車就衝開人群踱到我們面前了。
Nage chuan hei kanjian de xiang yuanchu da le yige hushao, yibu beijiu de changpeng mache jiu chongkai renqun duo dao women mianqian le.
The man in the black vest whistled afar, and an open carriage already waiting there pierced through the crowd and strolled towards us.

Example (7)

他沉重地頓了一下腳, 蹌踉地踱下土坡。
Ta chenzhong de dun le yixia jiao, qiangliang de duo xia tupo.
He stamped his foot heavily, and strolled unsteadily down the slope.

Example (8)

沿著馬路旁的便道, 我踉蹌地向前踱著。
Yan zhe malu pang de biandao, wo liangqiang de xiang qian duo zhe.
I strolled unsteadily forward on the pavement along the main road.

As in his translation of *Ulysses*, Xiao also uses such phrases as 跄踉地踱 or 踉跄地踱 in his creative writing. As a matter of fact, substituting the verb *zhuan* (paced) for *duo* in Example (5), *lai* (approached) in Example (6), or simply *zou* (walked) in Examples (7) and (8) would suit the context much better. It is very unusual in the Chinese language to use the verb *duo* to refer to the movement of a carriage pulled by horses, but Xiao uses it in Example (6) in his writing. In the translation of *Ulysses*, Xiao again uses it to modify the movement of a dog and a horse.

Example (9)

The retriever approaches sniffling, nose to the ground. (*U* 15.247)
一只能叼回獵物的狼狗, 鼻子貼地嗅著, 踱了過來。
Yizhi neng diao hui liewu de langgou, bizi tiedi xiu zhe, duo le guolai.

Example (10)

Too slow for Boylan, blazes Boylan, impatience Boylan, joggled the mare. (*U* 11.765–766)
母馬一顛一搖地向前踱著。對情緒亢奮的博伊蘭, 急不可待的博伊蘭來說, 真是太慢了。
Muma yidianyiyao de xiangqian duo zhe. Dui qingxu kangfen de boyilan, jibukedai de boyilan laishuo, zhenshi tai man le.

To testify to the unusualness of the collocation of *duo* with an animal, we compared the results against a RC, the large-scale corpus developed by the Center for Chinese Linguistics of Peking University (CCL of PKU). It contains 477 million Chinese characters, including 307 million modern characters and 170 million ancient characters, and the texts cover a wide range of sources, original and translated, literary and non-literary texts. We find that in the CCL corpus, only 7 occurrences of the 500 uses of *duo* are related to animals, including cattle ($f=4$), pigeons ($f=2$), and sparrows ($f=1$), as in Examples (11)–(16).

Example (11)

鴿子在中心廣場[踱]來飛去, 自由自在地覓食。
Gezi zai zhongxin guangchang duo lai fei qu, ziyouzizai de mishi.
On the central square pigeons were strolling and flying, freely seeking food.

Example (12)

傲慢的牛群毫不理會車鳴人催, [踱]步于路中央。
Aoman de niuqun haobulihui cheming rencui, duobu yu lu zhongyang.
Arrogant cattle strolled midway down the road, refusing to make way for the buzzing motors or the hastening crowds.

Example (13)

麗日晴空, 牧場青翠, 奶牛悠閒[踱]步。
Liri qingkong, muchang qingcui, nainiu youxian duobu.
The sun was bright, the sky clear, and the cows making their leisurely stroll on the verdant pasture.

Example (14)

水牛在田裏悠然[踱]著方步。
Shuiniu zai tian li youran duo zhe fangbu.
The buffalo was pacing leisurely in the field.

Example (15)

幾隻麻雀在草叢裏[踱]來[踱]去,青草茁壯成長。
Jizhi maque zai caocong li duo lai duo qu, qingcao zhuozhang chengzhang.
Several sparrows were pacing in the thick growing grass.

Example (16)

它們才掉過頭, 懶洋洋地向自己的圈棚[踱]去。
Tamen cai diao guo tou, lanyangyang de xiang ziji de juanpeng duo qu.
They would only then turn around and pace lazily toward their pens.

Although it is perhaps not inappropriate to use *duo* to describe the way of walking in the contexts of Examples (11)–(16), since the animals are all walking in a leisurely way, it would be very unnatural to use *duo* to describe the running of a retriever, in Example (9), and the joggle of a mare, in Example (10).

Of the 307 million modern Chinese words in the CCL, the total frequency of the word 踱 (*duo*) is 1986 occurrences. The frequency of the word word 踱 (*duo*) used in Xiao's translation (corpus 1) was then compared

Table 4 Chi-square of 踱 (*duo*) in the four corpora

Word	Freq. in corpus 1	Size of corpus 1	Freq. in corpus 2	Size of corpus 2	Chi-square	Significance (*p*)	
踱	72	500,000	5	520,000	60.9838	0.000***	+
Word	Freq. in corpus 1	Size of corpus 1	Freq. in corpus 3	Size of corpus 3	Chi-square	Significance (*p*)	
踱	72	500,000	48	230,000	4.0118	0.045*	–
Word	Freq. in corpus 1	Size of corpus 1	Freq. in corpus 4	Size of corpus 4	Chi-square	Significance (*p*)	
踱	72	500,000	1,986	307,317,000	1,412.3981	0.000***	+

Note Corpus 1 = Xiao's translation, Corpus 2 = Jin's translation, Corpus 3 = Xiao's writing, Corpus 4 = modern Chinese corpus of CCL. The asterisks (*) indicate significance level, and the '+' and '–' signs on the right-hand side indicate 'overuse' or 'underuse', respectively with that of the word in the other three corpora (Jin's translation, corpus 2; Xiao's own writing, corpus 3; and the CCL, corpus 4). More specifically, we performed a chi-square test, a procedure that measures whether a particular distribution of observed values is sufficiently different from an expected distribution to confirm that it is not a chance occurrence (Table 4).

The chi-square test shows that the differences are significant and that Xiao has a frequent tendency to use the word examined. Although we have examined only one word in detail, we can suggest that all the words in the wordlists generated by WordSmith Tools can evidence the particular preference of the two translators.[1] The study testifies to the existence and variation of translators' styles—the fingerprints metaphor that Baker (2000) posited. Moreover, the study also suggests that a text producer's habitual wording style in free writing may work its subtle influence on their translation, which could help to explain why different translators leave different fingerprints on their translations. It may be posited that, in transferring authorial ideas to the target readers, the translator consciously or subconsciously reverts back to their own language habits, and shows a tendency to use preferred expressions over other alternatives.

5 Translators' Styles Manifested in Syntactical Sequence

A translator's style is not only manifested at the lexical level, but also at the syntactic level. In Examples (11a) and (11b), the dependent clause 'because I was late' can be placed either before or after the independent clause 'they went without me'.

Example (11a)

<u>Because I was late,</u> they went without me.

[1]See Appendix for the top and bottom 60 items of the keyword comparison of the two translations.

Example (11b)

They went without me <u>because I was late.</u>

In the Chinese language, however, the position of clauses is more rigid: the dependent clause is normally placed before the independent clause. If the order is reversed, it would be interpreted as intending to achieve a rhetorical effect (Wang 2001: 233) because a post-positioned dependent clause weakens its own importance in the whole sentence. Compare the following two examples:

Example (12a)

<u>如果你不介意,</u> 我想提一個問題。
<u>Ruguo ni bu jieyi,</u> wo xiang ti yige wenti.
<u>If you don't mind,</u> I'd like to ask a question.

Example (12b)

我想提一個問題, <u>如果你不介意。</u>
Wo xiang ti yige wenti, <u>ruguo ni bu jieyi.</u>
I'd like to ask a question, <u>if you don't mind.</u>

Example (12a) assumes a normal, pre-positioned conditional clause, whereas Example (12b) takes on a post-positioned conditional clause, which functions as an add-on, hence its reduced importance.

When writing in Chinese as our native tongue, we may be quite conscious of the placement of clauses, so we may use this arrangement to achieve certain stylistic effects. In translation, however, we may not be always conscious of the weakened effect when we transfer the post-positioned clause to the target text. Checked against the source texts in the parallel corpora of *Ulysses*, it was found that the translations show some degree of similarity to the source text in post-positioned adverbial clauses. Examples (13b) and (13c) will suffice to show that the versions by both Xiao and Jin share a similar structure to the English original texts.

Example (13a)

——That's very interesting because that brother motive, don't you know, we find also in the old Irish myths. (*U* 9.956–57)

Example (13b)

——那非常有趣兒。因為, 要知道, 在愛爾蘭傳說中, 我們也能找到弟兄這一主題。
Na feichang youqur. Yinwei, yao zhidao, zai aierlan chuanshuo zhong, women ye neng zhaodao dixiong zhe yi zhuti.

Example (13c)

——很有意思, 因為我們在愛爾蘭古代神話中, 你們不知道嗎, 也看到這種兄弟題材的。
Hen you yisi, yinwei women zai aierlan gudai shenhua zhong, nimen bu zhidao ma, ye kandao zhezhong xiongdi ticai de.

We selected five conjunctions as nodes for an exhaustive search in the two translations: 如果 *ruguo* (conjunction of assumption), 只要 *zhiyao* (conjunction of condition), 儘管 *jinguan* (conjunction of concession), 雖然 *suiran* (conjunction of concession), and 因為 *yinwei* (conjunction of cause). We found that Jin's translation shows a higher degree of conformity to the English source text than Xiao's, in that as many as 40% of adverbial clauses are placed after the head nouns in Jin's translation, as opposed to 27.2% in Xiao's. Of the five items examined, the conjunction of cause, *yinwei*, is the most frequently post-positioned. This is especially obvious in Jin's translation, in which 180 out of a total of 284 instances where '*yinwei*' is used as a conjunction are post-positioned, accounting for 63.4%. Table 5 lists the frequency and percentage of post-positioned adverbial clauses in the translated texts.

When compared with his own writing, however, we find that Xiao uses 9.6% more post-positioned structures in his translation of *Ulysses*, as shown in Table 6.

Unlike lexical idiosyncrasy, the comparative study on the position of clauses reveals more similarity than divergence in the styles of the translators. It seems that both Xiao and Jin are influenced by the structure

Table 5 Frequency and percentage of post-positioned adverbial clauses in the translated texts

Items	Xiao's translation			Jin's translation		
	Post-position *f*	Pre-position *f*	% (post-position)	Post-position *f*	Pre-position *f*	% (post-position)
如果 ruguo	1	27	**3.6**	12	100	**10.7**
只要 zhiyao	1	58	**1.7**	4	56	**6.7**
儘管 jinguan	8	87	**8.4**	2	24	**7.7**
雖然 suiran	1	17	**5.6**	16	37	**30.2**
因為 yinwei	102	114	**47.2**	180	104	**63.4**
Total	113	303	**27.2**	214	321	**40.0**

Table 6 Frequency and percentage of post-positioned adverbial clauses in Xiao's writing and his translation

Items	Xiao's original			Xiao's translation		
	Post-position *f*	Pre-position *f*	% (post-position)	Post-position *f*	Pre-position *f*	% (post-position)
如果 ruguo	1	71	**1.4**	1	27	**3.6**
只要 zhiyao	2	26	**7.1**	1	58	**1.7**
儘管 jinguan	0	11	**0.0**	8	87	**8.4**
雖然 suiran	9	60	**13.0**	1	17	**5.6**
因為 yinwei	31	33	**48.4**	102	114	**47.2**
Total	43	201	**17.6**	113	303	**27.2**

of the source English text, leaving traces of foreignness in their translated texts, which marks the difference between a translation and a non-translation.

The much higher frequency of the post-positioned adverbial clauses in complex sentences in the translated text than in the original Chinese text discloses the interference of the source language structure in the process of translation. The presence of the foreign features as the result of the source language interference distinguishes the translated texts from the non-translated one in this case, which may be indicative of a broader trend in translation. Because of the distinctive features manifested in translated texts, translational language has been referred to as 'the third code' (Frawley 1984), 'the third language' (Duff 1981), and 'hybrid language' (Trosborg 2000). These terms reflect translation scholars' understanding about translation as a negotiation between the heterogeneity of the source language and the acceptability constraints of the target language. The finding also confirms Toury's 'law of interference', which suggests that 'in translation, phenomena pertaining to the make-up of the source text tend to be transferred to the target text'. The operation of this law, Toury surmizes, depends on the particular manner in which the source text is processed, the professional experience of the translator, and the socio-cultural conditions in which a translation is created (Toury 1995: 275–278).

6 Conclusion

This study of the Chinese translations of *Ulysses* has attempted to use an empirical methodology to look for factors that contribute to the stylistic features of the translated text, and to test the hypothesis that the translator leaves his own linguistic style in the translated text. Although 'difficult to spot' (Bernardini 2005), the analysis captures, to some extent, the behaviours of the translators, and suggests that a writer's habitual mode of linguistic expression manifested in free writing may also be found in their translation, which then may serve as evidence of the existence of the translator's fingerprints in their translations. On the syntactic level, the analysis finds that a translator's fingerprints leave traces of foreignness in the translated texts, which mark the difference between a translation and non-translated, original writing, revealing the interference of the source language structure on the translator. We therefore conclude that a translator's style in the translated text is a result of both the influence of his mother tongue and that of the source language. This helps explain the phenomenon that translations produced by different translators are different in lexical and syntactical styles, but that they are all expressed in a language somewhat different from the language of the original writing.

Appendix

Keyword comparisons of Xiao's and Jin's translations of *Ulysses* (The top and bottom 60 items)

	Key word	Freq.	%	RC Freq.	RC %	Keyness	*P*	Set
1	斯蒂芬	599	0.2	1		792.93	0	nr
2	啦	850	0.29	165	0.06	478.65	0	e
3	朝	288	0.1	21		264.02	0	p
4	迪达勒斯	168	0.06	0		226.02	0	nr
5	穆利根	164	0.06	0		220.64	0	nr
6	那	2512	0.85	1539	0.54	198.60	0	s
7	晓得	140	0.05	0		188.34	0	v
8	倘若	139	0.05	0		187.00	0	c
9	哦	157	0.05	5		173.73	0	e
10	乔	140	0.05	5		151.98	0	nr
11	利内翰	107	0.04	0		143.94	0	nr
12	跟	471	0.16	164	0.06	142.46	0	p
13	之	1052	0.36	549	0.19	140.86	0	r
14	彼	249	0.08	48	0.02	140.80	0	r
15	就	1915	0.65	1202	0.42	136.93	0	d
16	勃克	109	0.04	1		136.67	0	nr
17	地	2336	0.79	1543	0.54	132.79	0	u
18	个	1235	0.42	699	0.25	129.45	0	q
19	怎样	131	0.04	9		122.28	0	d
20	般	229	0.08	48	0.02	121.21	0	k
21	替	97	0.03	1		120.76	0	p
22	要么	94	0.03	1		116.78	0	c
23	迪格纳穆	85	0.03	0		114.34	0	nr
24	大家	143	0.05	17		108.30	0	r
25	市民	117	0.04	9		105.40	0	nr
26	所	530	0.18	237	0.08	103.08	0	p

(continued)

	Key word	Freq.	%	RC Freq.	RC %	Keyness	*P*	Set
27	有着	76	0.03	0		102.23	0	v
28	乃	88	0.03	2		102.05	0	v
29	坎宁翰	74	0.03	0		99.54	0	nr
30	西茜	74	0.03	0		99.54	0	nr
31	被	505	0.17	227	0.08	97.13	0	p
32	利奥波德	79	0.03	1		96.95	0	nr
33	康米	71	0.02	0		95.51	0	nr
34	兜里	68	0.02	0		91.47	0	f
35	没	293	0.1	100	0.04	91.20	0	d
36	摩莉	67	0.02	0		90.13	0	nr
37	曾	292	0.1	101	0.04	89.15	0	d
38	哩	172	0.06	38	0.01	87.07	0	e
39	然而	322	0.11	121	0.04	86.50	0	c
40	朝着	76	0.03	2		86.49	0	p
41	当中	63	0.02	0		84.75	0	f
42	相互	62	0.02	0		83.40	0	r
43	喏	95	0.03	8		82.97	0	e
44	当	315	0.11	123	0.04	79.34	0	p
45	能够	81	0.03	5		77.95	0	vd
46	博伊兰	57	0.02	0		76.67	0	nr
47	笃笃	55	0.02	0		73.98	0	o
48	嘛	116	0.04	19		73.48	0	e
49	鲍尔	70	0.02	3		73.42	0	nr
50	一道	79	0.03	6		71.46	0	d
51	或	349	0.12	153	0.05	70.71	0	c
52	帕特	51	0.02	0		68.60	0	nr
53	西蒙	51	0.02	0		68.60	0	nr
54	遂	50	0.02	0		67.26	0	d
55	踱	72	0.02	5		66.98	0	v
56	也罢	56	0.02	1		66.69	0	e
57	科尼	47	0.02	0		63.22	0	nr
58	巡警	53	0.02	1		62.76	0	n
59	英镑	57	0.02	2		62.06	0	q
60	卡弗里	46	0.02	0		61.88	0	nr
…		…	…	…	…	…	…	…
231	似的	119	0.04	211	0.07	−29.98	0	k
232	坎肩	3		33	0.01	−30.52	0	n
233	酒店	17		64	0.02	−31.05	0	n
234	愿	29		85	0.03	−31.13	0	vd
235	倒霉	3		34	0.01	−31.78	0	v
236	处	101	0.03	191	0.07	−32.09	0	f
237	如	109	0.04	204	0.07	−33.41	0	c

(continued)

	Key word	Freq.	%	RC Freq.	RC %	Keyness	*P*	Set
238	说话	28		86	0.03	−33.41	0	v
239	女士	12		57	0.02	−33.80	0	n
240	肯定	10		53	0.02	−34.03	0	d
241	是	4726	1.6	5096	1.8	−34.20	0	v
242	手中	8		49	0.02	−34.52	0	f
243	同时	36	0.01	101	0.04	−34.89	0	t
244	见到	26		86	0.03	−36.44	0	v
245	忘	19		74	0.03	−37.09	0	v
246	小心	5		44	0.02	−37.28	0	an
247	无	133	0.05	245	0.09	−38.54	0	v
248	站住	16		70	0.02	−38.88	0	v
249	那时	17		74	0.03	−40.93	0	t
250	不	1953	0.66	2288	0.81	−42.60	0	d
251	罗	3		43	0.02	−43.28	0	n
252	牧师	12		66	0.02	−43.45	0	n
253	模样	6		52	0.02	−43.77	0	n
254	脑袋	45	0.02	128	0.05	−45.06	0	n
255	许多	10		63	0.02	−45.12	0	m
256	种	142	0.05	271	0.1	−46.56	0	v
257	为何	4		49	0.02	−47.01	0	d
258	全	47	0.02	135	0.05	−48.14	0	d
259	是否	22		93	0.03	−50.18	0	v
260	铜	7		60	0.02	−50.26	0	n
261	找	87	0.03	201	0.07	−51.28	0	v
262	祈祷	14		78	0.03	−51.78	0	v
263	鼻头	4		53	0.02	−52.12	0	n
264	唷	13		79	0.03	−55.39	0	e
265	眼光	4		56	0.02	−55.98	0	n
266	知道	169	0.06	326	0.12	−57.47	0	v
267	如果	28		112	0.04	−57.54	0	c
268	呀	198	0.07	365	0.13	−57.55	0	e
269	了	4841	1.64	5393	1.9	−58.25	0	U
270	现在	109	0.04	245	0.09	−59.47	0	T
271	一点	85	0.03	210	0.07	−60.04	0	M
272	不错	12		83	0.03	−62.63	0	V
273	可以	184	0.06	359	0.13	−65.01	0	Vd
274	但是	64	0.02	186	0.07	−67.38	0	C
275	一些	109	0.04	259	0.09	−69.41	0	M
276	其	127	0.04	286	0.1	−69.67	0	R
277	已经	141	0.05	318	0.11	−77.69	0	D
278	J	14		101	0.04	−77.93	0	Nx
279	何	24		128	0.05	−82.54	0	N

(continued)

	Key word	Freq.	%	RC Freq.	RC %	Keyness	*P*	Set
280	一	3935	1.33	4616	1.63	−87.67	0	M
281	内	71	0.02	224	0.08	−89.91	0	F
282	人	1287	0.44	1747	0.62	−90.97	0	N
283	一个	808	0.27	1200	0.42	−94.55	0	M
284	口袋	11		110	0.04	−98.21	0	N
285	而	557	0.19	920	0.32	−106.17	0	C
286	看	338	0.11	647	0.23	−112.08	0	V
287	没有	330	0.11	663	0.23	−128.38	0	v
288	约	12		149	0.05	−143.61	0	Nr
289	或是	35	0.01	229	0.08	−167.66	0	C
290	有	1326	0.45	2155	0.76	−236.80	0	V

References

Baker, M. (2000). Towards a Methodology for Investigating the Style of a Literary Translator. *Target, 12*(2), 241–266.

Bernardini, S. (2005). Reviving Old Ideas: Parallel and Comparable Analysis in Translation Studies—With an Example for Translation Stylistics. In K. Aijmer & C. Alvstad (Eds.), *New Tendencies in Translation Studies*. Göteborg: University of Göteborg.

Boase-Beier, J. (2006). *Stylistic Approaches to Translation*. Manchester: St. Jerome.

Chinese Academy of Social Sciences. (2002). *The Contemporary Chinese Dictionary* (Chinese–English ed.). Beijing: Foreign Language Teaching and Research Press.

Duff, A. (1981). *The Third Language: Recurrent Problems of Translation into English*. Oxford: Pergamon Press.

Frawley, W. (1984). Prolegomenon to a Theory of Translation. In W. Frawley (Ed.), *Translation: Literary, Linguistic, and Philosophical Perspectives* (pp. 159–175). London and Toronto: Associated University Presses.

Granger, S., Lerot, J., & Petch-Tyson, S. (2007). *Corpus-Based Approach to Contrastive Linguistics and Translation Studies*. Beijing: Foreign Language Teaching and Research Press.

Jin, D. (1997). *Tran. Ulysses*. Beijing: People's Literature Publishing House.

Jin, D. (2001). *Shamrock and Chopsticks*. Hong Kong: City University of Hong Kong Press.

Kenny, D. (2001). *Lexis and Creativity in Translation: A Corpus-Based Study*. Manchester: St. Jerome.

Laviosa, S. (2002). *Corpus-Based Translation Studies*. Amsterdam: Rodopi.

Malmkjær, K. (2004). Translational Stylistics: Dulcken's Translations of Hans Christian Andersen. *Language and Literature, 13*(1), 13–24.

Marco, J. (2004). Translating Styles and Styles of Translating: Henry James and Edgar Allan Poe in Catalan. *Language and Literature, 13*(1), 73–90.

Mauranen, A. (2000). Strange Strings in Translated Language: A Study on Corpora. In M. Olohan (Ed.), *Intercultural Faultlines* (pp. 119–141). Manchester: St. Jerome.

Olohan, M. (2004). *Introducing Corpora in Translation Studies*. London and New York: Routledge.

Toury, G. (1995). *Descriptive Translation Studies and Beyond*. Amsterdam and Philadelphia: John Benjamins.

Trosborg, A. (2000). Translating Hybrid Political Texts. In A. Trosborg (Ed.), *Analysing Professional Genres* (pp. 145–158). Amsterdam: John Benjamins.

Xiao, Q. (2005 [1994]). *Tran. Ulysses*. Nanjing: Yilin Press.

Wang, D. (2001). *Modern Rhetoric*. Shanghai: Shanghai Foreign Language Education Press.

Exploratory and Critical Approaches to Corpus-based Translation Studies

Representing China in Translations of Two Korean News Outlets: A Corpus-based Discourse Analysis Approach

Tao Li

1 Introduction

The construction of a national image has recently become one of the prominent themes in translation studies, as shown in recent studies (Gu 2018; Kim 2017; Lee 2015; Li and Xu 2018; van Doorslaer et al. 2016). Originating from comparative literature, image studies focuses on the features of countries and people in accordance with the ways in which they are portrayed in literary works (Beller 2007: 7). Naturally, the investigation of national image building through translation is largely limited to the genre of fiction (e.g. Frank 2007; Hung 2005; Lee 2015). As many other disciplines introduce different theoretical perspectives to examine image building (e.g. Baker et al. 2013; Wang 2015)—such as politics, linguistics, international relations—image studies has also become increasingly cross-disciplinary. Research into

T. Li (✉)
Centre for Corpus Research,
Shanghai Ocean University, Shanghai, China
e-mail: tli@shou.edu.cn

K. Hu and K. H. Kim (eds.), *Corpus-based Translation and Interpreting Studies in Chinese Contexts*, Palgrave Studies in Translating and Interpreting,
https://doi.org/10.1007/978-3-030-21440-1_7

the presentation of national images in translation thus also extends from literary works to other genres, such as news, and the methods adopted for this kind of research are also not limited to the macro analysis of 'the selection of topics' (van Doorslaer 2012: 1054) but, rather, move to the empirical quantitative examination of the linguistic representations of national image. For example, drawing on a corpus-based discourse analysis approach, Kim (2013) carried out an investigation of the articles on North Korea from *Newsweek* and *CNN* and their Korean translations to identify the ways in which North Korea is discursively represented in Korean translated news. Interestingly, her analysis reveals that North Korea appears in the Korean target texts actively to exert some control in negotiations with the US, while North Korea is portrayed as a voiceless passive party in the English source texts. Similarly, Kemppanen (2004) carried out a corpus-based contrastive analysis of the word *ystävyys* (friendship) in Russian–Finnish translations and original (non-translated) Finnish texts on Finnish political history. The investigation of the collocations, word clusters, and actantial structure of the word *ystävyys* shows that, while the original Finnish texts present a negative semantic prosody of *ystävyys*, Finnish translations somehow project the positive cooperating actors for a common goal of friendship, which displays an unusual national image of the Soviet Union in translation.

Caimotto (2016) examined the image of Italy in 135 pieces of translated news in Italian, which were originally published in the UK newspaper *The Times* from 1969 to 1980. The analysis shows that, in English news, the collocates of 'Italy' that are endowed with negative semantic prosody are often translated into Italian words with positive or neutral semantic prosody, which results in some criticism of Italy being mitigated, while positive remarks on it are foregrounded. The research method adopted to examine the collocates of 'Italy' in Caimotto's study is helpful for the present study in terms of the investigation of China's image. With a similar research method, Kim (2017) examined the ways in which China is discursively represented in Korean translations of the news reports on China from *Newsweek* from 2005 to 2015. The patterns revealed through her analysis show that Korean news outlets tend to choose materials for translation that describe China as a rival superpower challenging the primacy of the US. It is also found that the

Korean news outlet under investigation tends to keep away from certain views in the English source texts and re-voice statements in certain articles from its own perspective by employing subtle linguistic devices whenever the criticisms of China are too strong.

Previous studies are conducive to this chapter, particularly in terms of methodology, but some issues of national image in translation are still not fully addressed. First, national images constructed in the translations of non-literary texts still remain rarely discussed, particularly when dealing with the language of Chinese. Second, most previous studies are still based on a macro analysis; also, among these few empirical studies, most either lack sufficient data or lack a systematic framework for a micro-linguistic analysis. Lastly, but also importantly, most studies that investigate the national image of China in translation are set in the context of English-speaking countries, with very little attention to China's national image in East Asian countries, although China's political relations with Asian countries has recently begun to get stronger and more visible, as can be seen in the example of the Asian Infrastructure Investment Bank and the North Korean issue. This chapter, therefore, departs from the previous studies to adopt a corpus-based discourse analysis approach in order to identify China's national image in the Chinese translations of the news articles provided by South Korean news outlets. Specifically, it aims to identify the ways in which China is portrayed in Chinese translations of the news reports on Terminal High Altitude Area Defense (THAAD) deployment from two South Korean news outlets with different orientations.

2 Corpus-based Discourse Analysis

Language is socially determined; and, as a social practice, discourse cannot be isolated from the context where it is produced, diffused, and consumed. Discourse analysis—in particular, critical discourse analysis—aims to reveal the meanings hidden in texts, focusing on the relationship between language and power, and the relationship between language and ideology (Fairclough 1989: 17).

However, discourse analysis, traditionally relying on introspection and theoretical deduction, has long been under severe criticism. One of the typical criticisms is that discourse analysts often subjectively choose certain linguistic features and investigate them in a small number of texts to confirm their assumption, thereby failing to avoid personal bias (e.g. Stubbs 1997; Widdowson 2004: 102). This criticism is countered, as Chilton et al. (2010) suggest, either with an acknowledgement of an analyst's position by arguing that no research is absolutely objective and all studies are somehow subservient to the researcher's personal interests; or with research relying on a large collection of data to illustrate their assumptions, rather than one or a few texts.

Against this background, a corpus-based approach has become a new direction in discourse analysis. As Baker (2006: 10) argues, one of the advantages of the corpus-based approach to discourse analysis is that it can help reduce the researcher's personal bias, because the analysis of a large collection of texts helps to avoid a researcher's subjective selection of texts and, thus, the result of the analysis can be more representative. Hunston (2002: 109) also points out that the corpus investigation of linguistic features has much to offer to discourse analysts in revealing ideology that is implicitly coded behind overt statements and in challenging established common sense. Similarly, Baker (2006: 1) argues that this approach can help uncover linguistic patterns that help researchers make sense of the ways that language is used in constructing discourses (or ways of constructing reality). Another advantage may be that, based on statistical data analysis, it supports repeatability, making the findings more reliable. In recent years, the corpus-based approach has repeatedly been applied to discourse analysis, as shown in Baker et al. (2013), Baker and Balirano (2017), and Fetzer (2014).

3 Data

Two South Korean news outlets were chosen to retrieve the data: *The Chosun Ilbo* (hereafter *Chosun*) and *The Hankyoreh* (hereafter *Hankyoreh*). *Chosun*, founded in 1920, is one of the major right-wing newspaper outlets in South Korea with a daily circulation of more than

Table 1 The THAAD corpus

Time	News outlets	Tokens
Pre-THAAD	*Chosun*	984
(8 January 2016–7 July 2016)	*Hankyoreh*	5093
Post-THAAD	*Chosun*	622
(8 July 2016–8 January 2017)	*Hankyoreh*	6851

1.8 million copies across the nation.[1] Its website is also available in English, Japanese, and Chinese.[2] *Hankyoreh*, though it claims to be 'the first newspaper in the world truly independent of political power and large capital', is one of the mainstream left-wing media in South Korea. It also provides its service in English, Japanese, and Chinese.[3]

On 8 July 2016, South Korea made a final decision, together with the US, to deploy THAAD in South Korea to counter North Korea's missile threat. This decision triggered wide concerns. China, which backed tough United Nations sanctions against North Korea after its nuclear test and a long-range rocket launch, has fiercely objected to THAAD deployment in South Korea, arguing that THAAD can be used to monitor the movements of its military within China and that the deployment would further destabilize the region. Since the THAAD issue marks a change in China–South Korea political relations from being intimate to icy, a corpus was built that covers all the news reports on THAAD from the online Chinese versions of both *Chosun* and *Hankyoreh*. The time when THAAD was deployed in South Korea was selected as a dividing line to identify whether the two news outlets were consistent in their ways of projecting China before and after THAAD deployment, and to examine whether they construct differing national images of China in relation to the THAAD issue. Table 1 shows the details of the THAAD corpus.

---

[1]https://about.chosun.com/files/brochure_e_2017.pdf (last accessed 23 May 2018).

[2]http://www.chosun.com/ (main page, Korean version), http://www.chosunonline.com/ (Chinese version), http://www.chosunonline.com/ (Japanese version), http://english.chosun.com/ (English version) (last accessed 23 May 2018).

[3]http://www.hani.co.kr/ (main page, Korean version), http://china.hani.co.kr/ (Chinese version), http://japan.hani.co.kr/ (Japanese version), http://english.hani.co.kr/ (English version).

The procedures for collecting data were as follows. First, 中国 (China) and 中方 (China's side) were chosen as search items with which to retrieve those concordance lines that describe China in the coverage of THAAD reports. Second, using the corpus software package WordSmith (version 6.0), all the collocates of the search items were generated with the purpose of identifying the lexical items that potentially illustrate attitudes towards China. Third, the list of all collocates appearing on the right-hand side of the search items was re-sorted by frequency in order to examine the patterns of China's reactions to THAAD deployment. The collocates on the right-hand side of the search items were chosen because syntactically, in Chinese, the agent of these collocates is 'China'; thus, this choice made it possible to observe the ways China reacted to the deployment of THAAD. Fourth, these collocates were categorized into a number of groups on the basis of either countries or persons, on the one hand, or the feelings or behaviours of China, on the other hand. Lastly, all the collocates were investigated within their context to examine how they represented the evaluative stance of the two news outlets.

4 Results and Discussion

4.1 *Chosun* Prior to THAAD Deployment

Before the deployment of THAAD, the countries collocating with the search item 'China' in *Chosun*'s coverage include South Korea, North Korea, Russia, and the US. Two key figures are also included: Xi Jinping, the President of China, and Kim Jong-un, the leader of North Korea. Both 'South Korea' and 'North Korea' co-occur with 'China' more than 10 times (South Korea, f=14; North Korea—including two occurrences of 'Kim Jong-un', f=9). However, Russia and the US—who, in the current political climate of the issue, also show their interest—only appear three times and twice, respectively, in China's collocates list. This may suggest that *Chosun* demonstrates that South Korea, North Korea, and China are the key players in the issue. However, detailed investigation of the search item in a larger context beyond the concordance line reveals that *Chosun* focuses on the conflict China has with both South Korea and North Korea, but mostly with South Korea, as 'South Korea' co-occurs with 'China' mainly in the context of China's opposition to the deployment of THAAD. It also shows that China is in conflict with North Korea because of China's dissatisfaction with North Korea's nuclear experiments and China's loss of control over North Korea. This dissatisfaction is reflected in the concordance line where 'China' collocates with 'Kim Jong-un', the current leader of North Korea, as can be seen from the concordance line:

> 据悉，本次 核试验 使 中国 对 金正恩 政权 的 绝望 感 增加
> It is said that this experiment makes China despair more of the Kim Jong-un's governance.[4]

However, according to *Chosun*, China's conflict with South Korea is due to North Korea's repeated nuclear experiments, which led South Korea to decide to deploy THAAD. *Chosun* constructs a discourse showing that South Korea is not to blame, as the direct factor that changed the current state of the Korean Peninsula is North Korea's nuclear tests, which makes China's opposition to South Korea's deployment of THAAD groundless. It also implies that China should blame North Korea for causing the trouble, rather than causing conflict with South Korea.

The analysis of the collocate list also has shown that both positive and negative comments are made about China; however, there are more negative comments. Only three cases positively describe China, including 重视 (take it seriously; f=2). For example:

> 目前 中国 最 **重视** 周边 国 外交
> China *takes seriously* its diplomatic relations with its neighbouring countries

[4]The translations of all the examples in this chapter are from the corresponding English websites of the two Korean news outlets.

中国 领导班子 极为 **重视** 由于 朝鲜 核试验 而 感受 到 地震 的 东北地区 人民 的 愤怒 和 网民 的 批评。
Chinese leadership *takes seriously* the anger of the people in China's north-east area and criticism of netizens because of the earthquake caused by the nuclear experiment of North Korea.

Both of these extracts are quoted from a Chinese scholar—Su Hao, a consultant for China's policies on the Korean Peninsula, who works in the China Foreign Affairs University, a university directly under the Ministry of Foreign Affairs of China. This implies that China is probably starting to take the issues in the Korean Peninsula seriously, including the nuclear issues of North Korea. Another positive example is 加强 (strengthen; f=1) in the concordance line:

中国 将 与 韩国 **加强** 合作，寻找 朝鲜 核 问题 的 方案
China will *strengthen* cooperation with South Korea to look for the solution to the North Korean nuclear issue.

It is again quoted from Su. From the context, it can be seen that Su Hao, a key figure in China's think tank for the issue, holds the view that:

目前 中国 最 重视 周边 国 外交，在 此 情况 下，朝鲜 正在 成为 最大 挑战
North Korea is becoming the largest challenge to China's development of its diplomatic relationships with its neighbouring countries.

All these extracts show that *Chosun*'s discourse about the issue is that even China was dissatisfied with North Korea and started to re-evaluate its diplomatic relations with it, a positive sign for South Korea.

There are a further two collocates of China—反对 (oppose; f=3) and 协助 (assist; f=4)—that negatively present China in the context. Among them is 协助, which is positive in its connotational meaning; however, it only occurs in relation to presumption. For example:

> 前任 青瓦台 高层人士 表示: '如果 在 这样 的 情况 下, 不能 好好 得到 中国 的 **协助**, …… 我们 应该 拿出 所有 能 拿出 的 牌, 要求 中国 协助。
> the former top officer in Blue House expressed that '**if** in this situation, we still can't get China's *assistance*, … we should take out all the cards that we have to require China to assist'.

反对 is used twice to show China's opposition to the deployment of THAAD and once to display China's opposition to imposing sanctions against North Korea. These words show a negative attitude to China because of China's opposition to South Korea's deployment of THAAD, which is aimed at protecting its people, and China's unwillingness to work together with the international community to pressure North Korea into ceasing nuclear tests.

There are more words that indicate criticism of China, such as 导致 (cause; f=2), 挑衅 (provoke and offend; f=2). 导致 is used in the context that China is a source of threat to the security of South Korea. For example:

> 我们 不能 忘记 2013 年末 中国 单方面 宣布 防空 识别区 **导致** 韩国 安保 受到 巨大 威胁 的 情况。
> We will never forget that at the end of 2013, China's unilateral declaration of air defense identification zone *causes* that the security of South Korea is under great threat.

The use of 挑衅 to collocate with China displays a clear criticism of China, as this word itself indicates a negative attitude. 一直 (always; f=2) in the collocation list is actually not a word that implies a very clear attitude, yet it is endowed with a negative meaning from the perspective of South Korea, together with the use of 'non-active attitude', as shown in the following example:

> 有 分析 认为, 朴槿惠 之所以 拿出 '萨德牌' 对 中国 施压, 是因为 最近 在 对 朝 制裁 的 局面 中, 中国 **一直** 持 不 积极 的 态度。

> It is analyzed that the reason why Park Geun-Hye plays a card of 'THAAD' to impose pressure on China is because, towards the recent sanctions against North Korea, China always takes a non-active attitude.

Another interesting word is 拥有 (possess; f=2). Though it is generally positive in connotation, it projects a negative sense in the context, such as the following concordance line:

> 中国 是 **拥有** 200 多 颗卫星 的 宇宙 强国, 也 是 拥有 将 周边国家 划入 射程 范围 之内 打击 手段 的 军事 强国 与 核 强国。 这样 的 中国 指责 为 应对 朝核 而 部署 在 韩国 的 雷达 的 探测 能力, 在 媒体 上 像 训斥 小孩 一样 警告 说 ' 韩国 要 慎重 为 之', 这 分明 是 无视 公平性 的 大国 逻辑。
> China is a powerful country that **possesses** more than 200 satellites and a military and nuclear power that also takes its neighbouring countries within its striking scope. However, China still rebukes South Korea for its deployment of radar with powerful detection to deal with North Korea's nuclear weapons as if China is criticizing a little kid publically in media, 'South Korea should be cautious about it [deploying THAAD]', which is the big country's logic that ignores fairness.

This concordance line implies a hypocritical image of China by arguing that, while China possesses many powerful weapons and its neighbouring countries are within striking range, it does not allow those neighbouring countries, including South Korea, to deploy a defensive system to protect themselves. The image of China that *Chosun* projects is that China uses its power to control neighbouring countries.

The word 担忧 (worry about; f=1) collocates with 'China', but the detailed analysis of the concordance line shows that it is actually from an interview by Thomas Shannon, the then US Under Secretary of State for Political Affairs, who said:

> 萨德 是 一种 防御 系统, 我 不 明白 中国 为何 **担忧** 它。
> THAAD is a defensive system. I don't understand why China *worries about* it.

It can be argued that, by quoting the expert's interview, *Chosun* tries to highlight the fact that THAAD is a defensive system, which is not intended to target China, and thus China's opposition is groundless.

All these examples suggest that the discourse *Chosun* constructs about THAAD is that the deployment of THAAD is a rational and correct response from South Korea to North Korea's provocative nuclear experiment, while casting China as critical concerning what is a necessity to South Korea. Given the fact that the translated discourse targets a Chinese audience, it is reasonable to presume that what *Chosun* was trying to achieve is not only the negative presentation of China, but also the conveying of a message to Chinese readers that it is an understandable and necessary choice made by the South Korean government to deploy THAAD.

4.2 *Chosun* After THAAD Deployment

After the deployment of THAAD, countries that co-occur with 'China' in the coverage of *Chosun* are 'North Korea' (f=5), 'South Korea' (f=5), and the 'US' (f=2). Compared with the coverage of *Chosun* prior to the deployment of THAAD, it seems that there is a more frequent collocation between China and North Korea. Another difference is that Russia is no longer in the collocation list of 'China'.

The collocation between 'China' and 'North Korea' illustrates three points. One is questioning China's unwise protection of North Korea as shown in:

> 即便 韩国 放弃 了 萨德, 中国 也 不会 就 对 **朝鲜** 施压 足以 动摇 其 体制 的 压力, 以 实现 无核化
> even if South Korea gives up THAAD, China will never impose enough pressure on *North Korea* to change its regime and realise denuclearization

This indicates that China would not take decisive measures to solve the issue of North Korea's nuclear tests, and implies that China's laissez-faire attitude to North Korea's development of nuclear weapons has indirectly caused the deployment of THAAD, a rational and necessary measure for South Korea to protect itself. Another point is the conflict between China and North Korea as shown in the concordance that reads:

> 中国 想 拉拢 **朝鲜**, 朝鲜 却 总是 瞎 搅合。
> China wants to draw near to *North Korea*, but North Korea is yet always making a mess.

The last point is China's strategy to take North Korea as a card to play in competing with the US. For example, one concordance line where China and North Korea co-occur reads:

> 和 美国 进行 霸权 竞争 的 中国, 分明 是 将 **朝鲜** 的 核武器 当做 自己 国家 的 资产。
> China that competes with the US in hegemony clearly takes *North Korea*'s nuclear weapon as China's own national assets.

This contrasts with the pattern identified in the analysis of the coverage of *Chosun* prior to the deployment, where the collocation between 'China' and 'Russia' occurs twice, but both focus on one topic: the visit to China by Russia's President Putin. This collocation displays the close relationship between China and Russia as shown in a concordance line that reads:

> 时隔 两天 再次 见面, 展示 了 对 美 联合阵线 的 巩固。
> another meeting after two days shows the consolidation of the united front against the US.

However, after the deployment, 'Russia' does not show up in combination with 'China'. One interesting agent in the analysis of Chinese translations of news articles produced by *Chosun* both before and after the deployment period is Lotte Co., Ltd, one of the big conglomerates in South Korea. 'Lotte' does not co-occur with 'China' in the coverage of *Chosun* prior to the deployment of THAAD, but occurs twice together with 'China' thereafter. These two cases of the collocation between 'China' and 'Lotte' are in the context that China suddenly inspects Lotte branches in China as though in retaliation against this company because Lotte provides its premises for the deployment of THAAD in South Korea.

There are some other collocates indicating China's concerns about the deployment of THAAD. Such words in most cases are actually a criticism of China, such as 担心 (worry; f=2). One co-occurrence with 'China' is to display China's worry about the deployment of THAAD, but the other is a warning to the South Korean government as is in the context that:

> 在 中国 的 威势 和 胁迫 面前， 韩国 是 选择 成为 一个 自主 独立 的 国家? 还是 ...... 因为 **担心** 饭碗 出 问题 就 干脆 选择 放弃 生命 和 安全?
> in front of China's puissance and intimidation, will South Korea choose to be an independent country or ...*worrying about* the problem of employment so as to giving up life and security?

Both cases of 过激 (drastic; f=2) occur in the quotation of a Chinese scholar, Prof. Ma Yong at Beijing Normal University, one of the leading universities in China, who argues that China is too drastic in its response to the deployment of THAAD and who is criticized later as a mole or traitor to China in the Chinese media.[5] Because this is quoted from a Chinese scholar, such information suggests that, in China, there are differing viewpoints on the issue of THAAD. It thus might indicate to the Chinese audience, as well as the South Korean, that there is a voice even in China that accepts the deployment of THAAD, which lends legitimacy to the South Korean government's decision. 不满 (unsatisfactory; f=1) and 气恼 (angry; f=1) are a further two words that reflect China's feelings about and attitudes towards the issue. However, the description that China is unsatisfied with the deployment

[5]http://www.focustt.com/2016/0815/35689.shtml (last accessed 6 March 2018).

of THAAD and angry about the South Korean government actually occurs in the context that the deployment of THAAD is:

中国 对朝 政策 的 必然结果，也 是 自作自受。
the inevitable consequence of China's policies to North Korea, and China deserved it.

There are also certain other lexical items describing China's acts. For example, 想要 (want; f=2) co-occurs with 'China' in two contexts. One is in the concordance line:

如果 中国 **想要** 的 伙伴关系 是 以 韩国 放弃 主权 为 前提 的，韩国 就 没 必要 有所 留恋，也 没 必要 担心 关系恶化。
if the partnership with South Korea that China *wants* is on the condition that South Korea gives up sovereignty, South Korea doesn't have to feel reluctant to break up with China, and doesn't have to worry about the relationship getting worse.

This means, in one sense, that it is an 'if' (i.e. a supposition) and, in another sense, that China does not care about its partner's core interest in an established relation, only its own. The other lexical item is in:

如果 中国 不 **想要** 萨德 就 应 让 朝鲜 弃核。
If China does not *want* THAAD, China should make North Korea give up its nuclear weapons.

This is, again, in one sense a presumption, but it indicates China's unfairness worrying about its own safety but not caring about the threat that North Korea poses to South Korea. Both cases of 拉拢 (draw near to; f=2) describe China's drawing near to North Korea. One context is that:

有 分析 认为，这 是因为 在 南海 判决 中 完败 、 韩 半岛 部署 萨德 等，让 中国 更 需要 **拉拢** 朝鲜

some analyst thinks that China's failure in arbitration of the South China Sea and the deployment of THAAD in Korean peninsula make China in more need of *drawing near to* North Korea

This line also covers another word: 需要 (need), which shows that THAAD is not the only reason that China is getting closer to North Korea. This concordance also shows that China is in conflict with many other countries and is becoming isolated from neighbouring countries, so it now needs to be closer to North Korea, a country that is considered a rogue state by many countries. It is also implied that, to some extent, South Korea stands with the majority. The other example is that:

中国 想 **拉拢** 朝鲜, 朝鲜 却 总是 瞎 搅合。
China wants to *draw near to* North Korea, but North Korea is yet always making a mess.

This shows that *Chosun* highlights an unwise image of China because China still wants to have a relationship with North Korea somehow, a country that always behaves abnormally and makes trouble.

It thus can be argued that, although the coverage of *Chosun* after THAAD deployment makes China a focus, it still projects China as a country that is indifferent to the security of its neighbours. This news outlet also indicates that China's concerns—no matter whether these are worrying, drastic, unsatisfactory, or angry—either have no grounds, or are deserved as the consequence of its irresponsible acts.

4.3 *Hankyoreh* Prior to the Deployment

Before the deployment of THAAD, the countries that co-occur with China in the Chinese translations of the coverage of *Hankyoreh* from the highest to the lowest frequency are North Korea (f=16), the US (f=16), South Korea (f=10), and Russia (f=7). The list also contains some figures: Wang Yi (f=12), Xi Jinping (f=6), and Park Geun-Hye (the former president of South Korea; f=1). Interestingly, it also contains the United Nations (f=2). Compared with the coverage of

Chosun within the same time span, the biggest difference is that 'China' co-occurs more often with the 'US', which suggests that *Hankyoreh* considers the THAAD issue in relation to these two countries. The Chinese President and Chinese Minister of Foreign Affairs are frequently mentioned, which to some extent indicates that they, the Chinese side, are given more space and voice in the coverage. The interesting co-occurrence of 'China' with the 'United Nations' may be due to the following two reasons: one is the fact that China is a permanent member of the United Nations Security Council, and the other is that China supports the sanctions on North Korea approved by the Security Council. The one co-occurrence of South Korean President Park with China is in the context where:

> 美国 第一个 时间段 搬出 '中国 责任 论' 对 中国 施压, 紧接着 **朴槿惠** 总统 宣布 考虑 部署萨德, 也 被 认为 是 对华 施压 之 举。 中国 究竟 做错 了 什么?
> The U.S. immediately claimed 'China's responsibility' to impose pressure on China. Following it, President Park declared the deployment of THAAD, which is considered as a sign to impose pressure on China. What on earth has China done wrong?

The second sentence in this example shows that the article actually says Park's decision to deploy THAAD is unfair to China, which is far from what *Chosun* argues.

The collocates identified in the vicinity of 'China' in this corpus, which reflect China's acts, can be grouped into three categories: (i) China's attitude to the deployment of THAAD; (ii) China's reaction; and (iii) China's conflicts with South Korea, the US, and, surprisingly, North Korea. First, when it comes to the collocates that present China's attitude to the deployment, lexical items such as 反对 (oppose; f=12), 强烈 (strongly [oppose]); f=6), 敏感 (sensitive; f=2), and 忌讳 (taboo/sth unacceptable; f=2) are identified, all of which describe China's opposition to South Korea's decision. These collocates clearly demonstrate China's strong opposition to the deployment and indicate that China takes it as a sensitive issue and a taboo subject. A further collocate, 不会 (will not; f=3), illustrates China's determination in its stance towards the deployment, as shown in the following extended concordance line:

> 中方 **不会** 坐视 半岛 稳定 受到 根本 破坏, 不会 坐视 中方 的 安全 利益 受到 无端 损害。
> China *will not* ignore the damage to the stability of the Peninsula as well as China's security interest.

Both Wang Yi, the Minister of Foreign Affairs of China, and Hua Chunying, the spokeswoman of the Ministry, are also given voices to illustrate that the deployment of THAAD in South Korea harms China's 正当 (legitimate or proper; f=2) interest.

Second, in terms of the collocates that present China's reaction to the issue of THAAD, the word 制裁 (sanction; f=19) is one of the top collocates. The examination of the extended concordance lines shows that 'sanction' is used to describe China being pushed into imposing sanctions against North Korea, or China being hesitant to sanction North Korea. 撤资 (withdraw investment; f=5) from South Korea is another collocate that describes China's action on the issue. It is worth noting that 逐渐 (gradually; f=3) and 加快 (quicken; f=2) are used to modify 撤资 (withdraw investment). Another collocate 提高 (improve; f=3) is used to describe that China is improving its capacity for dealing with the issue, which could be interpreted as a warning to the South Korean government. Lastly, regarding the collocates that illustrate China's efforts to solve North Korea's launch of missiles, 推动 (push forward; f=2) is identified: a closer look at the extended concordance lines reveals that 推动 is used to show that China tries to persuade the parties involved in solving the problem through negotiation.

The last category of collocates illustrates China's conflicts with other countries, mostly with the US and South Korea. First, China's 安全 (security; f=8), 利益 (interest; f=7), and 战略 (strategy; f=5), are endangered and harmed. 造成 (cause; f=3) and 很大 (very big; f=3) are used to show that the deployment of THAAD causes a very big threat to China. For example:

萨德 的 核心 — — X 波段 雷达 的 探测 半径 超过 3000 公里，这会 对 中国 的 安全 **造成 很大** 的 威胁。
X-band radar, the core of THAAD, has a detection radius of more than 3,000 kilometres. This *causes* a *very big* threat to China's security.

The other two words, 展开 (carry out; f=2) and 施压 (impose pressure; f=5), are used to report that the US and South Korea are exerting pressure on China. For example:

美国 已经 开始 对 中国 **展开** 全方位 **施压**。
The US has started *carrying out* pressure on China in all domains.

韩美 两国政府 正 全方位 向 中国 **施压**，要求 提高 对朝 制裁 水平。
South Korean and the US governments are *imposing pressure* on China in all domains, requiring China to raise the level of sanction against North Korea.

Interestingly, there are two cases of 威胁 (threat; f=4) that co-occur with 'China' expressing the threat to China from North Korea. For example:

中朝 两国 拥有 长达 1300 公里 的 边境线，如果 朝鲜 成为 中国 的 '敌对 国家'，其 对 中国 的 威胁 程度 有 可能 远高于 '拥核' 的 朝鲜 对 中国 的 **威胁**。
China and North Korea has a borderline of 1,300 kilometres. If North Korea becomes a hostile country of China, its *threat* to China is much higher than a North Korea possessing nuclear weapon

恶化 (deteriorate; f=2) also illustrates this point, as shown in the following concordance line:

朝鲜 第三轮 核试验 之后 中国 不惜 **恶化** 与 朝鲜 的 关系，严格执行 了 联合国安理会 的 制裁 决议。

> After the third nuclear experiment, China, regardless of relationship *deterioration* with North Korea, implements strictly the sanction resolution of the Security Council of the UN.

Overall, the general picture in the coverage of *Hankyoreh* prior to THAAD shows that China strongly opposes the deployment of THAAD and will take action to protect China's interests. It also shows China's hesitation to cooperate with the other parties to sanction North Korea, which suggests that China is forced to draw near to North Korea even though China once strictly abided by the resolution of the Security Council to sanction North Korea. Other measures that China may take also include China's withdrawal of its investment in South Korea and China's efforts to solve the nuclear experiment of North Korea through negotiation. From the analysis, it can be seen that *Hankyoreh* displays a sympathetic attitude to China: the decision made by the US and South Korea to deploy THAAD harms China's proper interest, and places China under great threat and pressure.

4.4 *Hankyoreh* After the Deployment

The countries that collocate with 'China' in the coverage of *Hankyoreh* after the deployment of THAAD include 'South Korea' (f=26), 'Russia' (f=17), the 'US' (f=13), 'North Korea' (f=7), and 'Japan' (f=3). The striking difference between *Hankyoreh* before and after the deployment lies in: (i) a rise in the frequency for 'China' and 'Russia'; (ii) that 'China' collocates more frequently with 'South Korea' than it does with 'North Korea'; and (iii) 'China' co-occurring with 'Japan', which never occurs in other subcorpora under investigation. An in-depth analysis of the extended concordance lines and their contexts reveals that China and Russia are allied, because both are against the deployment of THAAD, arguing that it is a surveillance system used by the US, not South Korea, to oversee China and Russia, as shown in the news entitled '中国:一旦威胁到我们, 将即刻进行攻击' (China: As soon as we are threatened, we will launch attack immediately). In the news, it is analysed that:

> 中国 和 **俄罗斯** 认为 美国 在 韩国 部署 萨德 破坏 了 地区 与 全球战略 平衡, 做出 了 强烈 反对。
> both China and *Russia* are against the deployment of THAAD because the US' deployment of THAAD in South Korea breaks the regional and global balance.

The news also said that:

> 美国 在 欧洲 和 亚洲 构建 导弹 防御 体系, 形成 了 对 俄罗斯 的 夹击
> The missile defence system the US established in Europe and Asia poses attack on Russia from both sides

and

> 中国 的 安全 一旦 受到 威胁, 将 立刻 发起 打击, 中国 与 **俄罗斯** 拥有 一切 打击 手段。
> As soon as China's security is under threat, China will launch attack immediately. China and *Russia* have all means of attack.

The collocation of 'China' and 'Russia' in the coverage of *Hankyoreh* suggests that this issue will not end in China but, rather, will continue to grow. It can also be interpreted as a warning that China, allying with Russia, could counter any threats and would launch damaging attacks on South Korea if THAAD threatens China.

The analysis of the collocates in the Chinese coverage of *Hangyoreh* before the deployment of THAAD shows that no great difference has been found in terms of 'China' co-occurring with 'South Korea' and 'North Korea'. However, the analysis has shown that, after the deployment, there is a sudden rise in the collocation of 'China' with 'South Korea', which can be attributed to the fact that the conflict or tension between China and South Korea were increasing immediately after the event. The co-occurring pattern between China and South Korea centres on two issues: (i) China strongly opposing South Korea's decision to deploy THAAD; and (ii) China, as South Korea's largest trading partner, imposing economic sanctions against South Korea. This suggests that *Hankyoreh* is projecting a worrying stance towards the deployment of THAAD on South Korean soil, arguing that it will cause China's economic retaliation, as China once did to Japan, as shown in the concordance line:

> 2010 年 钓鱼岛 事件 之后， 日本 对 中国 的 出口 和 投资 以及 访日 中国 游客量 全部 骤减， 中国 的 第一 进口国 由 **日本** 变成 了 韩国。
> After the Diaoyu Islands issue in 2010, Japan's export to and investment in China and the number of China's visitors to Japan all sharply fell, and Korea replaced *Japan* as the first exporting country to China.

The three co-occurrences of 'China' and 'Japan' also focus on two topics: (i) China's efforts to solve the issue, such as efforts to resume the Six-party Talks, a negotiation mechanism that China set up to solve the nuclear issue of North Korea, and China's participation in the meeting of Foreign Ministers of China, Japan, and South Korea; and (ii) South Korea did not actively participate in but, rather, was dragged into the alliance with the US and Japan against China as in the context of signing the General Security of Military Information Agreement between South Korea and Japan. It is reported in *Hankyoreh* after THAAD deployment that:

> 但 该 协定 内容 若 放到 风雨飘摇 的 东北亚 安全 环境 内 来看 就 另当别论 了。 美国 东北亚 霸权 战略 的 目标 便是 要 封锁 正在 崛起 的 中国， 日本 事实上 也 将 中国 看做 是 一大 威胁， 从而 不断扩大 自卫队 的 活动 范围， 而 美日 自然 想要 将 韩国 拖入 这一 对华 战线 中。
> But it would be a different story if the agreement were to be seen in the precarious security environment of Northeast Asia. The goal of the US' hegemony strategy in Northeast Asia is to block rising China, and Japan in fact also sees China as a big threat, expanding the operational scope of its Self Defence Forces. So the US and Japan naturally want to drag South Korea into the frontline against China.

An interesting item that collocates with 'China' is 'Seongju', the county in North Gyeongsang Province, South Korea, where THAAD was planned to be deployed. All three cases of 'Seongju' are from quotations from Theodore Postol, a professor and expert in missile defence systems at the Massachusetts Institute of Technology in the US. He argues in the interview that, if China attacks Seongju, the consequence will be even worse than that of Hiroshima, a Japanese city that was destroyed by a US nuclear weapon during World War II, which led to Japan's surrender. Quoting the expert who actually compares the THAAD issue with the Hiroshima case is such a strong warning that it would be likely to make South Koreans reconsider their decision. It can therefore be argued that this news outlet is constructing a discourse that the decision to deploy THAAD can also be a serious blow to South Korea.

It is also worth mentioning three agents who were identified in the collocation list of the *Hankyoreh* after the deployment corpus: Xi Jinping, Wang Yi, and Lotte. 'Xi Jinping' and 'Wang Yi' occur 8 and 15 times, respectively, which is even higher than their frequency before the deployment. This, to some extent, implies that the representatives of China are given more space to express China's opposing attitudes towards the deployment of THAAD. Similar to *Chosun*, 'Lotte' (f=2) is included in the collocation list of 'China', which also shows China's economic retaliatory reaction to South Korea's decision, though China argues that it is a routine inspection. It thus can be argued that *Hankyoreh*'s voice concerning the deployment of THAAD in South Korea is negative because of China's strong opposition, possible military attack from both China and Russia, the economic retaliation from China, and even the Korean people's opposition, particularly those people in Seongju.

For the collocates that reflect China's behaviour, the coverage of *Hankyoreh* after the deployment is focused on China's strong opposition and China's reaction to the decision. 反对 (oppose; f=19) becomes one of the top collocates in the collocation list of 'China'. There are also two words in the list that are used to modify 反对: 强烈 (strongly; f=9) and 坚决 (resolutely; f=4). China is also described as an actor who takes measures to retaliate against South Korea. 报复 (retaliate; f=6), 批判 (berate; f=5), and 攻击 (attack; f=1) are used to display China's reaction to the deployment. An example of this can be seen in the concordance line that explains the possibility that China will *attack* Seongju if China is under threat. Other interesting lexical items include 制裁 (sanction; f=3), a phrase used to explain China's inspection of the Korean company Lotte, which is considered as 赤裸裸 (undisguised; f=2) retaliation against South Korea. All these reflect China's get-tough policy dealing with the issue, as the following concordance line shows:

> 应 将 政策 的 重心 由 '对朝 制裁' 转向 '对 韩 制裁'
> China should transfer the focus of its policy from 'sanction on North Korea' to 'sanction on South Korea'

One interesting point is that, unlike *Chosun*, *Hankyoreh* seems to suggest that it is the US, Japan, and South Korea that caused the THAAD issue and China's conflicts with South Korea. This can be illustrated through the collocation list of 'China'. 强行 (force; f=2) shows that the US and South Korea *force* the deployment of THAAD. 造成 (cause; f=2) indicates that the deployment of THAAD *cause*s China's security crisis, and harm to the security interest of South Korea's neighbouring countries, particularly China and Russia. Other lexical items such as 威胁 (threat; f=5), 施压 (impose pressure; f=3), express that China is under threat and pressure from the US and Japan. For example:

> 在 正式 与 中国 讨论 联合国 制裁 之前，美国 对 中国 和 朝鲜 进行 高强度 **施压**。
> Before discussing the UN sanction, the US has *imposed* highly intense *pressure* on China and North Korea.

In general, *Hankyoreh* is not in favour of the idea of the deployment of THAAD, and highlights that the deployment has aroused strong opposition not only from both neighbouring countries, but also from people in South Korea, and that this opposition, particularly from China, has resulted in serious economic consequences. It also attempts to construct the discourse that China is not to blame for the consequences and the reaction is reasonable, in that China is under threat because of the deployment of THAAD approved by the US and South Korea.

5 National Interest First: A Geopolitical Account

Geopolitics is apparently one of the factors that affect news reports (Kim et al. 2007). It influences many aspects of the production of news, such as how the topics are chosen and how news discourse is structured, both of which acts finally project a political stance, or the voice of a particular party. The deployment of THAAD in South Korea, from its proposal to its landing, aroused a series of heated discussions both in and out of the country, and became a great crux of diplomacy in East Asia.

According to Lee (2016), the dilemma that South Korea faced was that it has to sacrifice economic interests for its security, or vice versa. The Park administration seemed to lose the political balance between its long-time ally, the US, to which it was existentially bound, and its neighbour and biggest trade partner, China. If it cooperates with the US to deploy THAAD directed at North Korea and, potentially, China, it risks conflict with China, a neighbouring country and its largest trade partner.[6] However, if it does not deploy THAAD, it faces a nuclear threat from North Korea, a threat that cannot be removed by China but can be lifted by cooperating with the US.

Politically, for any state, national interest is the ultimate objective, and is vital and irreplaceable (Njoku 2001: 128). Even in democratic countries that ensure freedom of the press, news outlets are sensitive to the national interest, no matter whether they are leftist or rightist. As McQuail (1992: 241) argues, 'the mass media, in their normal operation, tend to be rooted in a nexus of unexplicated attachment to the "the national interest" and to the values of patriotism'. However, due to common backgrounds and interests, people of a certain group reach an agreement to influence public opinion so as to guarantee the interests of individual members of the group. Appeals for different interests eventually lead to the emergence of a variety of voices. In a democratic society

[6]According to *Country Report on Trade* (data available from 2008) issued by the Ministry of Commerce of China, China became the largest trade partner of South Korea in 2008. https://countryreport.mofcom.gov.cn/new/view110209.asp?news_id=8163 (last accessed 20 June 2018).

such as South Korea, where its Constitution guarantees freedom of speech for its citizens and media, it is clear that there are various voices in terms of the deployment of THAAD, and all claim to protect the national interests of South Korea.

Since 8 July 2016, when the South Korean government agreed to work closely with the US to deploy THAAD, it encountered both support and opposition, both at home and abroad.[7] Internationally, the US and Japan are sincere supporters of the deployment of THAAD to combat the North Korean nuclear threat. Apart from China's repeated warnings, Russia, as a geopolitical adversary to the US, also strongly objected the deployment of this military radar system and declared that not only may it reach Russian territory, but it also poses a threat to the existing military balance in the Korean Peninsula.[8] Large demonstrations and protests for and against the deployment of THAAD across South Korea show that different voices were heard and different views were put forward within the country, too. Similarly, different news outlets have different political orientations and different views on societal issues. *Hankyoreh* and *Chosun* are the two typical cases.

The analysis has shown that *Hankyoreh* presented China as a neighbouring country that has close economic links with South Korea. *Hankyoreh* also portrayed China, together with the South Korean people, as a victim of THAAD deployment, explaining that THAAD puts China's national security under threat from the US and that it is not surprising to see China's retaliation to South Korea. It also argues that the deployment of THAAD would probably lead to serious military and economic consequences, which would take a toll on South Korea.

Before the THAAD issue, the political and economic relationship between China and South Korea entered a honeymoon phase. When the then South Korean president Park Geun-Hye came into office, she took a series of steps to improve the relationship with China. As a neighbouring country, China has been South Korea's largest trade

[7]http://english.hani.co.kr/arti/english_edition/e_national/756532.html (last accessed 20 June 2018).

[8]https://www.cbsnews.com/news/why-thaad-is-controversial-in-south-korea-china-and-russia/ (last accessed 20 June 2018).

partner. In 2013, bilateral trade volumes between South Korea and China reached 274.2 billion US dollars, surpassing the size of trade that South Korea conducted with Japan and the US combined.[9] The warmth in South Korean relations with China was not limited to the economic sphere, but was also evident in the political and social sphere, as shown in Park's presence at China's seventieth anniversary of the end of World War II. Park was offered a reception of a high standard where she was placed on the left of the host, President Xi, and to her right was seated Russian President Putin. Similarly, Xi also paid a state visit to South Korea before visiting North Korea, violating the practice that Chinese presidents have always visited North Korea first, to signify China's traditional tie with North Korea. Such an altered and evolved political relationship between the two countries also ensures a significant increase in their economic ties. Under such circumstances, the Park administration is certainly willing to continue the close cooperation with China. Such a government stance is reflected in *Hankyoreh*'s reports.

On the other hand, *Chosun* highlights that China is against South Korea's rational decision to deploy THAAD as self-defence against a potential nuclear threat from North Korea, and argues that South Korea needs to further cooperate with its reliable ally, the US. *Chosun*'s stance towards China can also be traced by reference to geopolitical evidence. Since the Korean War (1950–1953), the Korean Peninsula has been a place of geopolitical conflicts and a part of the continued cold war (Kim 2006). South Korea and North Korea, though formerly one nation, consider each other as the enemy, and both have a national government department especially for the reunification of the Korean Peninsula. Since Kim Jong-un became the leader of North Korea in 2012, he has adopted a new strategy to further strengthen the quality of nuclear weapons, which has increased tensions on the Korean Peninsula.[10] Despite a series of sanctions from the Security Council of the United Nations, North

[9]http://www.chinatoday.com.cn/ctchinese/economy/article/2014-08/06/content_633421.htm (last accessed 20 June 2018).

[10]http://www.xinhuanet.com/english/2016-03/04/c_135154908.htm (last accessed 20 June 2018).

Korea has continued its nuclear tests. North Korea's nuclear weapon tests and missile launches, from the perspective of South Korea, constitute a serious threat to the national security of South Korea. However, China, as a traditional ally of North Korea, could not restrain North Korea even though China repeatedly declared its firm stance on the denuclearization of the Korean Peninsula. Even at the time of the G-20 meeting held in China, where President Park met President Xi to seek China's cooperation in dealing with North Korea's threat, North Korea fired three medium-range ballistic missiles into the sea off its east coast.[11] China's failure to stop North Korea's nuclear programme pushed South Korea, a traditional ally of the US, to further integrate into the US security system. It seemed to South Korea that THAAD deployment was a necessary measure to safeguard its national security and the lives of its people, and it was thus considered reasonable to deploy THAAD to enhance South Korea's defence system against North Korean nuclear threats and to protect South Korea's national interest. *Chosun* reports display the validity of the South Korean government's decision to deploy THAAD, a decision made to protect South Korea and its people.

So, it can be seen that the democratic political system in South Korea allows different voices on THAAD deployment and geopolitical influences on China in various Korean news outlets, but national interest is still the bottom line for these news reports. For example, according to South Korea's National Security Law, speeches in favour of the North Korean government or communism can be punished. The South Korean government also imposes strict censorship on online materials, such as contents positively presenting North Korea, or denouncing the South Korean or US governments.[12] As Haggard and You (2015: 167) mention, South Korea's freedom of the press status was downgraded from 'free' to 'partly free' by Freedom House in 2010, who reached a similar conclusion with respect to internet freedom in 2011[13]:

[11]https://www.theguardian.com/world/2016/sep/05/north-korea-fires-three-ballistic-missiles-into-sea-reports (last accessed 20 June 2018).

[12]https://opennet.net/research/profiles/south-korea (last accessed 20 June 2018).

[13]See also https://rsf.org/en/ranking/2017 (last accessed 20 June 2018).

'Governments on both the political right and left have placed limits on freedom of expression in order to contain the political opposition' (Haggard and You 2015: 168). So, news outlets in South Korea, though endowed by their Constitution with the rights of a free press, have to set national interest as their top principle when reporting, willingly or unwillingly. Though *Chosun* and *Hankyoreh* present different attitudes towards China in their reports on THAAD deployment, their base line of reports is South Korea's national interest.

6 Conclusion

News reporting is one of the main means to construct a national image; thus how a news outlet represents a national image in its reports represents its stance towards that country. The examination of the ways in which the national image of a country in a news report is discursively constructed, particularly in the media of another country through translation, could help reveal the stance of the news outlet. It is argued that geopolitical relations between the related countries have an impact on the production of the news reports, and national interest always has top priority in news reports in a country with complex geopolitical relations. The projection of China in South Korean news outlets provides another starting point for further analysis of national image in the translations of news reports.

As the analysis shows, *Chosun*, the major right-wing newspaper, and *Hankyoreh*, the mainstream left-wing newspaper in South Korea, project China in different ways in a small corpus of Chinese translations of news reports on THAAD deployment in South Korea. The stances of the two news outlets towards China are kept consistent before and after the deployment of THAAD. Generally, *Chosun* portrays China as a country that lacks willingness to be actively involved in imposing sanctions against North Korea, even when it is evident that North Korea is threatening world peace. It thus argues that South Korea's deployment of THAAD is a rational and necessary response to North Korea's provocative nuclear threats. Conversely, *Hankyoreh* reports paint a different picture, where China is depicted as a close economic partner and a military power that could work together with Russia to take actions against the deployment of THAAD. It also describes China's retaliation against THAAD deployment as understandable, highlighting the potential threat to China's national interest from the US and its allies. The corpus analysis reveals very different voices and narratives about one issue.

As the data in this study are limited, it would be interesting to examine how the Korean media project China over a longer period from a diachronic perspective. Another possibility for the study of national image in future research would be to analyse the linguistic features of the national image within a systematic framework, extending from collocation in a small corpus to the combination of a more theoretically analytical framework and technically big data driven quantitative analysis.

Appendix: Collocate Lists of 'China' (Including the Tokens 中国 and 中方)

Collocates	Relation (MI)	Total right	Collocates	Relation (MI)	Total right	Collocates	Relation (MI)	Total right
Collocate list of 'China' in the coverage of *Chosum* prior to THAAD deployment								
韩国	10.97	14.00	应该	1.44	2.00	安保	10.32	1.00
中国	4.27	8.00	态度	2.52	2.00	对外	4.18	1.00
媒体	5.24	8.00	战略	1.98	2.00	对象	2.75	1.00
对	0.65	7.00	抗战	4.93	2.00	屏蔽	9.74	1.00
朝鲜	6.68	7.00	拥有	2.99	2.00	强调	2.40	1.00
外交	6.26	5.00	挑衅	6.93	2.00	总统	3.51	1.00
主席	3.78	4.00	方面	1.02	2.00	想法	3.80	1.00
做出	4.28	4.00	检疫	9.74	2.00	成为	0.17	1.00
协助	5.22	4.00	检验	4.07	2.00	批评	4.52	1.00
国家	1.06	4.00	活动	0.41	2.00	报复	5.57	1.00
如果	2.00	4.00	立场	5.57	2.00	报纸	3.44	1.00
将	0.54	4.00	美国	0.73	2.00	报道	2.63	1.00
监督	3.53	4.00	胜利	3.07	2.00	担忧	5.93	1.00
质量	2.32	4.00	行动	2.02	2.00	指出	2.39	1.00
习近平	9.74	3.00	选手	4.18	2.00	推进	1.07	1.00
以	0.11	3.00	重视	2.43	2.00	提出	0.75	1.00
俄罗斯	5.80	3.00	防空	8.74	2.00	政策	1.20	1.00
前	0.52	3.00	韩	5.09	2.00	敏感	3.81	1.00
反对	5.04	3.00	导致	0.86	2.00	本身	2.66	1.00

Collocates	Relation (MI)	Total right	Collocates	Relation (MI)	Total right	Collocates	Relation (MI)	Total right
施压	9.32	3.00	领导班子	7.74	2.00	杂志	4.18	1.00
而	0.07	3.00	不是	7.28	1.00	正式	3.05	1.00
进行	0.82	3.00	为了	0.99	1.00	由于	0.85	1.00
问题	1.32	3.00	亲属	5.57	1.00	的	0.95	1.00
一直	0.92	2.00	以及	0.63	1.00	目的	2.27	1.00
之后	1.49	2.00	使	0.98	1.00	真正	2.50	1.00
但	0.34	2.00	加强	0.85	1.00	积极	1.08	1.00
作为	0.39	2.00	半岛	7.36	1.00	绝望	4.57	1.00
金正恩	0.23	2.00	南海	7.74	1.00	行为	0.88	1.00
促进	1.20	2.00	合作	2.14	1.00	表明	2.75	1.00
关系	1.41	2.00	商讨	6.74	1.00	谈话	5.78	1.00
内心	2.93	2.00	国事访问	9.74	1.00	连	1.26	1.00
北京	2.09	2.00	国务委员	8.74	1.00	部署	4.00	1.00
却	0.29	2.00	坚决	3.61	1.00	部长	3.83	1.00
可能	0.78	2.00	声音	1.67	1.00	问题	6.38	1.00

Collocates	Relation (MI)	Total right	Collocates	Relation (MI)	Total right
Collocate list of 'China' in the coverage of *Chosum* after THAAD deployment					
韩国	5.55	5.00	想要	1.95	2.00
反应	4.69	4.00	部署	4.74	2.00
外交	6.04	4.00	不满	5.22	1.00
政策	1.62	4.00	主张	3.88	1.00
朝鲜	5.42	4.00	令	2.27	1.00
乐天	11.32	3.00	原因	1.60	1.00
韩	4.68	3.00	反对	4.04	1.00
俄罗斯	5.22	2.00	因此	1.32	1.00
过激	9.15	2.00	如果	1.00	1.00
利益	2.00	2.00	感到	2.01	1.00
担心	3.98	2.00	愿	2.92	1.00
大于	5.22	2.00	损害	4.61	1.00
学者	3.29	2.00	日	2.27	1.00
应	0.96	2.00	是因为	7.42	1.00
战略	1.98	2.00	气恼	7.42	1.00
拉拢	4.57	2.00	称	2.27	1.00
美国	1.47	2.00	表征	6.74	1.00

Collocates	Relation (MI)	Total right	Collocates	Relation (MI)	Total right	Collocates	Relation (MI)	Total right	Collocates	Relation (MI)	Total right
Collocate list of 'China' in the coverage of *Hankyoreh* prior to THAAD deployment											
的	0.37	126.00	但	1.07	3.00	忌讳	7.15	2.00	因为	1.56	1.00
在	0.58	23.00	做出	4.28	3.00	态度	3.84	2.00	国内	1.94	1.00
制裁	10.27	19.00	全面	2.37	3.00	恶化	6.42	2.00	国际	0.15	1.00
与	2.14	16.00	其	0.48	3.00	成为	1.97	2.00	地区	1.38	1.00
朝鲜	7.90	16.00	则	1.27	3.00	抗议	5.65	2.00	增加	1.54	1.00
美国	4.51	16.00	北京	1.76	3.00	推动	1.31	2.00	声称	6.57	1.00
外交部长	11.06	13.00	参与	2.25	3.00	提出	2.92	2.00	大楼	5.15	1.00
中国	5.65	12.00	强化	4.65	3.00	摩擦	6.04	2.00	孤立	7.52	1.00
反对	6.85	12.00	强调	3.98	3.00	敌对	6.04	2.00	安保	9.74	1.00
王毅	10.65	12.00	很	0.21	3.00	敏感	3.81	2.00	对于	1.26	1.00
国家	2.55	11.00	很大	9.74	3.00	方面	0.44	2.00	导弹	7.00	1.00
对	1.11	11.00	总统	5.51	3.00	是否	2.62	2.00	导致	3.17	1.00
为	1.22	10.00	提高	1.18	3.00	更	0.80	2.00	封锁	7.00	1.00
和	0.11	10.00	数量	3.80	3.00	最为	3.93	2.00	局势	5.93	1.00
将	2.54	10.00	无效	6.86	3.00	最近	3.82	2.00	局面	3.69	1.00
韩国	7.32	10.00	曾	1.71	3.00	月	3.58	2.00	层面	3.33	1.00
也	0.67	8.00	等	0.22	3.00	朝	3.36	2.00	已	0.11	1.00
会	1.27	8.00	舆论	5.53	3.00	朴	8.15	2.00	已经	0.74	1.00
安全	3.34	8.00	逐渐	3.07	3.00	正	1.13	2.00	市场	0.93	1.00
部署	7.22	8.00	造成	3.13	3.00	正当	4.18	2.00	干涉	6.04	1.00
韩	6.90	8.00	针对	5.09	3.00	甚至	1.67	2.00	年末	8.74	1.00
上	0.09	7.00	预算	4.86	3.00	由	1.33	2.00	开始	1.43	1.00
主席	4.27	7.00	三年	9.74	2.00	看来	2.96	2.00	必要	2.67	1.00
俄罗斯	7.22	7.00	为了	1.58	2.00	矛盾	2.86	2.00	情况	2.40	1.00
利益	3.81	7.00	举行	3.07	2.00	程度	2.56	2.00	意味着	3.38	1.00
可能	3.01	7.00	也就是说	5.15	2.00	空军	5.42	2.00	报道	2.63	1.00
弹道导弹	11.74	7.00	人士	5.11	2.00	立刻	3.12	2.00	担心	3.98	1.00
习近平	10.32	6.00	们	0.90	2.00	结交	7.42	2.00	持续	2.38	1.00
并	1.01	6.00	价值	1.82	2.00	美	1.18	2.00	指出	2.39	1.00

Collocates	Relation (MI)	Total right	Collocates	Relation (MI)	Total right	Collocates	Relation (MI)	Total right	Collocates	Relation (MI)	Total right
强烈	5.04	6.00	会谈	7.74	2.00	联合国	3.86	2.00	措施	2.52	1.00
进行	1.99	6.00	传统	1.60	2.00	能够	1.83	2.00	改变	2.07	1.00
问题	1.85	6.00	使用	2.02	2.00	表现	1.50	2.00	旨在	6.08	1.00
半岛	8.36	5.00	公开	3.59	2.00	论	3.52	2.00	是	2.91	1.00
如果	2.17	5.00	共同	1.54	2.00	访问	5.85	2.00	是因为	7.42	1.00
战略	4.44	5.00	决议	6.52	2.00	试图	3.63	2.00	更是	6.28	1.00
施压	10.91	5.00	加入	3.28	2.00	负责	2.17	2.00	某	2.11	1.00
正在	4.50	5.00	加快	1.74	2.00	贸易	3.59	2.00	此	0.89	1.00
称	4.73	5.00	动向	7.15	2.00	越	3.03	2.00	民众	3.86	1.00
表示	4.37	5.00	动荡	6.15	2.00	过去	1.19	2.00	派遣	6.28	1.00
认为	2.68	5.00	去年	5.15	2.00	这样	0.73	2.00	特别	1.00	1.00
资本	4.97	5.00	反而	3.63	2.00	一直	1.50	1.00	现在	0.08	1.00
资金	3.42	5.00	发射	6.04	2.00	不仅	1.50	1.00	理念	3.25	1.00
都	0.19	5.00	发生	0.87	2.00	不会	14.16	1.00	用于	2.87	1.00
今年	2.70	4.00	受到	9.80	2.00	不能	2.65	1.00	的	1.53	1.00
关系	2.00	4.00	同盟	5.57	2.00	举动	5.15	1.00	目前	1.38	1.00
出现	2.11	4.00	向	1.41	2.00	介入	6.24	1.00	目的	2.27	1.00
化	2.15	4.00	周边	4.83	2.00	企业	1.01	1.00	相信	2.72	1.00
国防	5.45	4.00	因此	1.32	2.00	会晤	5.49	1.00	稳定	1.38	1.00
外交	6.45	4.00	国务卿	9.06	2.00	但是	0.28	1.00	第二年	9.74	1.00
外交部	8.06	4.00	坚持	8.45	2.00	保障	1.32	1.00	结束	2.74	1.00
大使	6.83	4.00	大陆	4.90	2.00	做法	3.76	1.00	结果	1.32	1.00
威胁	5.32	4.00	完全	2.12	2.00	公然	6.74	1.00	考虑	2.77	1.00
执行	4.47	4.00	完整	4.55	2.00	军事	3.94	1.00	股市	4.35	1.00
政策	1.62	4.00	宣布	3.76	2.00	利益	9.23	1.00	虽	2.78	1.00
核武器	7.74	4.00	对方	2.52	2.00	制约	3.76	1.00	观点	2.83	1.00
正式	4.05	4.00	对立	5.74	2.00	刺激	4.18	1.00	说明	2.36	1.00
海军	7.74	4.00	展开	4.65	2.00	前	0.52	1.00	责任	2.97	1.00
而	0.07	4.00	履行	3.63	2.00	加强	0.85	1.00	这些	0.58	1.00
要求	2.65	4.00	左	4.08	2.00	努力	1.87	1.00	这次	3.53	1.00

Collocates	Relation (MI)	Total right	Collocates	Relation (MI)	Total right	Collocates	Relation (MI)	Total right	Collocates	Relation (MI)	Total right
选举	3.69	4.00	希望	2.80	2.00	半岛	13.27	1.00	进入	1.64	1.00
驻	6.69	4.00	应对	4.35	2.00	南海	7.74	1.00	部长	4.83	1.00
一味	7.00	3.00	应该	0.86	2.00	原因	1.60	1.00	采取	2.98	1.00
一旦	4.53	3.00	当局	5.57	2.00	只要	2.00	1.00	难	1.29	1.00
不会	8.52	3.00	影响	1.40	2.00	合作	1.56	1.00	非常	1.53	1.00
主张	5.30	3.00	影响力	4.31	2.00	同时	0.77	1.00			
主权	5.86	3.00	彻底	3.61	2.00	吗	0.50	1.00			

Collocates	Relation (MI)	Total right	Collocates	Relation (MI)	Total right	Collocates	Relation (MI)	Total right	Collocates	Relation (MI)	Total right
Collocate list of 'China' in the coverage of *Hankyoreh* after THAAD deployment											
在	1.02	31.00	应该	1.86	3.00	担心	3.57	2.00	国际	0.74	1.00
韩国	8.23	26.00	建设	0.86	3.00	拒绝	3.47	2.00	图片	5.49	1.00
和	0.84	23.00	强化	4.91	3.00	拥有	2.41	2.00	在内	4.22	1.00
反对	7.62	19.00	当天	5.49	3.00	接受	2.82	2.00	处于	2.49	1.00
国家	3.38	19.00	当局	6.79	3.00	提及	6.04	2.00	外交部	7.32	1.00
中国	5.97	18.00	总统	5.51	3.00	政府	1.41	2.00	大陆	4.31	1.00
与	2.49	17.00	意见	3.74	3.00	政治	1.58	2.00	子公司	7.74	1.00
了	0.13	17.00	政策	1.62	3.00	文化	0.03	2.00	审判	6.86	1.00
俄罗斯	8.54	17.00	施压	9.74	3.00	是	2.91	2.00	宣布	4.76	1.00
将	2.91	16.00	日本	3.84	3.00	曾	2.71	2.00	对于	2.26	1.00
外交部长	11.06	15.00	时	0.31	3.00	月	8.35	2.00	对立	5.74	1.00
对	2.04	15.00	更	0.22	3.00	核	4.53	2.00	导致	3.17	1.00
并	2.60	15.00	未	2.63	3.00	正	0.55	2.00	就是	1.12	1.00
进行	3.21	15.00	朴	9.15	3.00	消费	2.78	2.00	屈辱	5.93	1.00
王毅	10.55	15.00	正在	4.86	3.00	用于	2.87	2.00	属于	3.16	1.00
美国	4.06	13.00	立场	6.57	3.00	立即	3.23	2.00	市场	0.93	1.00

Collocates	Relation (MI)	Total right	Collocates	Relation (MI)	Total right	Collocates	Relation (MI)	Total right	Collocates	Relation (MI)	Total right
部署	7.55	12.00	美	2.18	3.00	继	4.93	2.00	希冀	9.74	1.00
举行	6.07	11.00	联合国	4.28	3.00	能力	0.79	2.00	强调	3.72	1.00
也	0.99	11.00	舆论	5.11	3.00	行动	2.61	2.00	恶化	7.74	1.00
采取	4.98	11.00	星洲	7.83	3.00	西湖	6.93	2.00	成为	0.17	1.00
主席	5.37	9.00	被	0.67	3.00	观点	3.42	2.00	战略性	4.93	1.00
安全	3.34	9.00	讨论	3.73	3.00	解决	1.84	2.00	手段	3.07	1.00
强烈	5.50	9.00	部署	11.64	3.00	议员	8.74	2.00	打击	4.57	1.00
杭州	6.74	9.00	韩	5.09	3.00	记者	4.12	2.00	执行	2.88	1.00
中	0.54	8.00	首脑	7.52	3.00	访问	7.11	2.00	投资	1.21	1.00
习近平	11.32	8.00	一切	2.14	2.00	评判	6.93	2.00	指出	3.71	1.00
媒体	4.51	8.00	一方面	3.38	2.00	该	1.39	2.00	挑衅	6.93	1.00
方面	2.76	8.00	一致	4.23	2.00	贬值	7.74	2.00	推进	1.07	1.00
月	4.29	8.00	上海	1.87	2.00	资本	3.97	2.00	措施	9.74	1.00
等	1.74	8.00	不能	2.65	2.00	赤裸裸	7.42	2.00	攻击	4.15	1.00
南海	10.06	7.00	之前	2.07	2.00	达	2.12	2.00	教授	3.21	1.00
官方	7.83	7.00	之所以	3.74	2.00	过	0.48	2.00	敦促	9.74	1.00
朝鲜	6.90	7.00	乐天	11.32	2.00	迎接	4.69	2.00	旨在	5.49	1.00
而	1.19	7.00	也	4.58	2.00	这样	0.31	2.00	明确	2.91	1.00
认为	2.68	7.00	人民币	4.25	2.00	这种	0.88	2.00	最近	3.82	1.00
问题	2.15	7.00	人气	8.00	2.00	进一步	1.98	2.00	朝	2.94	1.00
之间	2.84	6.00	会	5.59	2.00	造成	2.13	2.00	期间	2.49	1.00
以及	2.80	6.00	但是	2.09	2.00	选择	1.85	2.00	束缚	5.65	1.00
利益	3.81	6.00	何种	6.28	2.00	采取	9.62	2.00	来源	4.01	1.00
可能	2.90	6.00	保护	2.09	2.00	重申	5.22	2.00	模式	1.52	1.00
报复	7.38	6.00	停止	4.31	2.00	防御	7.46	2.00	欢迎	3.72	1.00
的	3.27	6.00	共产党	3.93	2.00	顾问	6.00	2.00	此次	3.72	1.00
相关	3.24	6.00	具体	1.75	2.00	首先	2.05	2.00	武力	7.42	1.00
予以	4.95	5.00	再次	2.67	2.00	一直	0.92	1.00	民主党	8.74	1.00
二	1.62	5.00	则	1.27	2.00	上	4.73	1.00	民生	2.98	1.00
共同	2.86	5.00	利用	1.78	2.00	不仅	2.08	1.00	牵制	7.74	1.00

Collocates	Relation (MI)	Total right	Collocates	Relation (MI)	Total right	Collocates	Relation (MI)	Total right	Collocates	Relation (MI)	Total right
军事	5.11	5.00	反应	3.69	2.00	不满	5.22	1.00	犯难	9.74	1.00
及	1.64	5.00	反应	10.34	2.00	不顾	6.15	1.00	甚至	1.08	1.00
因此	2.32	5.00	召开	2.84	2.00	专家	2.26	1.00	电视	3.23	1.00
国内	3.26	5.00	可以	0.58	2.00	为了	2.31	1.00	百货商店	9.74	1.00
在野党	11.32	5.00	同时	1.36	2.00	主任	3.26	1.00	的话	4.22	1.00
威胁	5.91	5.00	同盟	6.57	2.00	之后	2.91	1.00	相当于	8.00	1.00
导弹	8.00	5.00	向	0.93	2.00	也就是说	3.83	1.00	称	10.08	1.00
战略	3.98	5.00	商量	5.74	2.00	事实上	3.76	1.00	约束力	7.15	1.00
批判	7.25	5.00	回避	5.65	2.00	们	1.63	1.00	结果	1.91	1.00
日	5.08	5.00	在	3.25	2.00	任何	1.51	1.00	能够	1.83	1.00
活动	1.73	5.00	地区	1.80	2.00	会议	2.01	1.00	自身	9.66	1.00
称	5.36	5.00	坚决	4.19	2.00	但	0.07	1.00	艺人	5.57	1.00
表示	4.76	5.00	坚决	10.84	2.00	体系	2.25	1.00	表明	3.34	1.00
驻	6.20	5.00	声明	5.57	2.00	做出	3.54	1.00	表现	1.50	1.00
为	0.43	4.00	大使	6.42	2.00	做法	3.76	1.00	要求	7.71	1.00
于	0.67	4.00	安理会	8.00	2.00	全面	1.37	1.00	计划	1.57	1.00
人民日报	5.22	4.00	审批	4.65	2.00	其	0.07	1.00	访华	5.93	1.00
关系	2.73	4.00	宪法	4.74	2.00	出口	2.86	1.00	评论	4.93	1.00
受到	3.57	4.00	对应	5.68	2.00	出席	4.83	1.00	评论家	7.42	1.00
合作	3.14	4.00	对此	10.32	2.00	出现	1.37	1.00	试图	3.63	1.00
吗	2.31	4.00	对话	3.83	2.00	出访	8.42	1.00	请求	4.98	1.00
因为	1.34	4.00	将	6.19	2.00	分裂	4.35	1.00	调整	1.85	1.00
外交	6.26	4.00	展开	3.65	2.00	副	2.09	1.00	调查	2.56	1.00
已经	0.74	4.00	峰会	4.72	2.00	加入	3.28	1.00	过去	1.19	1.00
应对	6.46	4.00	崛起	6.08	2.00	努力	1.87	1.00	连续	3.05	1.00
开始	1.92	4.00	左	4.08	2.00	北京	0.76	1.00	那么	1.30	1.00
所	0.47	4.00	序言	8.15	2.00	半岛	6.04	1.00	金	1.97	1.00
措施	4.10	4.00	引进	5.62	2.00	半岛	13.27	1.00	针对	4.92	1.00
提出	1.75	4.00	弹道导弹	10.32	2.00	即使	3.07	1.00	钓鱼岛	9.74	1.00
通过	2.13	4.00	强硬	7.42	2.00	压制	6.42	1.00	限制	3.50	1.00

Collocates	Relation (MI)	Total right	Collocates	Relation (MI)	Total right	Collocates	Relation (MI)	Total right	Collocates	Relation (MI)	Total right
不会	8.74	3.00	强行	5.83	2.00	原则	2.59	1.00	陷阱	6.42	1.00
主张	3.88	3.00	影响	1.72	2.00	原定	7.42	1.00	集团	2.54	1.00
主权	5.86	3.00	很大	9.32	2.00	参与	1.66	1.00	雷达	6.57	1.00
争端	7.74	3.00	必要	3.26	2.00	发射	6.04	1.00	需要	0.05	1.00
会	0.53	3.00	忧虑	6.32	2.00	取消	12.06	1.00	霸权	7.15	1.00
决定	3.13	3.00	态度	3.52	2.00	可能性	4.77	1.00	韩	11.32	1.00
制裁	7.15	3.00	总部	4.25	2.00	同样	2.26	1.00	高空	5.49	1.00
却	0.70	3.00	扩张	4.69	2.00	回应	4.93	1.00			
如果	1.81	3.00	报道	2.63	2.00	国务卿	7.74	1.00			

References

Baker, P. (2006). *Using Corpora in Discourse Analysis*. London: Continuum.

Baker, P., & Balirano, G. (2017). *Queering Masculinities in Language and Culture*. London: Palgrave.

Baker, P., Costas, G., & McEnery, T. (2013). *Discourse Analysis and Media Attitudes: The Representation of Islam in the British Press*. Cambridge: Cambridge University Press.

Beller, M. (2007). Perception, Image, Imagology. In M. Beller & J. Leerssen (Eds.), *Imagology: The Cultural Construction and Literary Representation of National Characters* (pp. 3–16). Amsterdam: Rodopi.

Caimotto, M. C. (2016). Images of Turmoil: Italy Portrayed in Britain and Re-mirrored in Italy. In L. van Doorslaer, P. Flynn, & J. Leerssen (Eds.), *Interconnecting Translation Studies and Imagology* (pp. 239–256). Amsterdam: John Benjamins.

Chilton, P., Tian, H., & Wodak, R. (2010). Reflections on Discourse and Critique in China and the West. *Journal of Language and Politics, 9*(4), 489–507.

Fairclough, N. (1989). *Language and Power*. London: Longman.

Fetzer, A. (2014). I Think, I Mean and I Believe in Political Discourse: Collocates, Functions and Distribution. *Functions of Language, 21*(1), 67–94.

Frank, H. (2007). *Cultural Encounters in Translated Children's Literature*. Manchester: St. Jerome.

Gu, C. (2018). Forging a Glorious Past via the 'Present Perfect': A Corpus-Based CDA Analysis of China's Past Accomplishments Discourse Mediat(is)ed at China's Interpreted Political Press Conferences. *Discourse Context & Media, 24*, 137–149. https://doi.org/10.1016/j.dcm.2018.03.007.

Haggard, S., & You, J.-S. (2015). Freedom of Expression in South Korea. *Journal of Contemporary Asia, 45*(1), 167–179.

Hung, E. (2005). *Translation and Cultural Change: Studies in History, Norms, and Image Projection*. Amsterdam: John Benjamins.

Hunston, S. (2002). *Corpora in Applied Linguistics*. Cambridge: Cambridge University Press.

Kemppanen, H. (2004). Keywords and Ideology in Translated History Texts: A Corpus-Based Analysis. *Across Languages and Cultures, 5*(1), 89–106.

Kim, H., Su, T.-Y., & Hong, J. (2007). The Influence of Geopolitics and Foreign Policy on the U.S. and Canadian Media: An Analysis of Newspaper Coverage of Sudan's Darfur Conflict. *International Journal of Press/Politics, 12*(3), 87–95.

Kim, K. H. (2013). *Mediating American and South Korean News Discourses About North Korea Through Translation: A Corpus-Based Critical Discourse Analysis* (Unpublished PhD thesis). University of Manchester.

Kim, K. H. (2017). Newsweek Discourses on China and Their Korean Translations: A Corpus-Based Approach. *Discourse, Context & Media, 15,* 34–44.

Kim, S. S. (2006). *The Two Koreas and the Great Powers*. Cambridge: Cambridge University Press.

Lee, B. (2016). THAAD and the Sino-South Korean Strategic Dilemma. *The Diplomat.* https://thediplomat.com/2016/10/thaad-and-the-sino-south-korean-strategic-dilemma/.

Lee, T. K. (2015). China as Dystopia: Cultural Imaginings Through Translation. *Translation Studies, 8*(3), 251–268.

Li, T., & Xu, F. (2018). Re-appraising Self and Other in the English Translation of Contemporary Chinese Political Discourse. *Discourse, Context & Media, 25,* 106–113.

McQuail, D. (1992). *Media Performance: Mass Communication and the Public Interest.* London: Sage.

Njoku, D. (2001). *Readings in Citizenship Education*. Enugu: John Jacob's Classic Publishers.

Stubbs, M. (1997). Whorf's Children: Critical Comments on Critical Discourse Analysis. In A. Ryan & A. Wray (Eds.), *Evolving Models of Language* (pp. 100–116). Clevedon: Multilingual Matters.

van Doorslaer, L. (2012). Translating, Narrating and Constructing Images in Journalism with a Test Case on Representation in Flemish TV News. *Meta, 57*(4), 1046–1059.

van Doorslaer, L., Flynn, P., & Leerssen, J. (Eds.). (2016). *Interconnecting Translation Studies and Imagology*. Amsterdam: John Benjamins.

Wang, N. (2015). Introduction of Rediscovering China: Interdisciplinary Perspectives. *European Review, 23*(2), 173–179.

Widdowson, H. (2004). *Text, Context, Pretext: Critical Issues in Critical Discourse Analysis*. Oxford: Blackwell.

Corpus-based Translation Studies and Translation Cognition Research: Similarity and Convergence

Kaibao Hu

1 Introduction

Since the 1990s, corpus-based translation studies (CTS) has undergone rapid development with the construction of a large number of bilingual parallel corpora and translational corpora for use in research on features of translation, translational norms, translators' style and translator training, and other related fields (Baker 1993; Laviosa 2002; Olohan 2004; Wang 2004, 2011). In recent years, corpora have increasingly been used in translation cognition research (TCR) to explore the properties and laws of the translation process (Alves and Vale 2011). However, CTS and TCR are considered to be two separate fields of study in mainstream academia, since the former focuses on the research on translation as a product, while the latter focuses on the research on translation as a process. This is evidenced by the fact that little attempt has been made to conduct TCR by using a corpus. This study, however, attempts to

K. Hu (✉)
Institute of Corpus Studies and Applications,
Shanghai International Studies University, Shanghai, China

K. Hu and K. H. Kim (eds.), *Corpus-based Translation and Interpreting Studies in Chinese Contexts*, Palgrave Studies in Translating and Interpreting,
https://doi.org/10.1007/978-3-030-21440-1_8

identify ways in which these two can converge, by examining the similarities and the contradictory or complementary features. To address these issues, this chapter, following a brief introduction to the main research areas of CTS and TCR, discusses in detail the similarities between CTS and TCR, and the implications and convergence of the two research fields.

2 The Similarities Between CTS and TCR

As noted, the main research areas of CTS include studies on features of translation, translator style, translational norms, translation process, and translator training. As Kruger (2002) puts it, CTS is a branch of the discipline that uses corpora of original and/or translated text for the empirical study of the product and process of translation. CTS also aims to reveal the nature of translation and translation process through the interplay of theoretical constructs and hypotheses, variety of data, novel descriptive categories, and a rigorous, flexible methodology. It can be applied in both inductive and deductive research, as well as product-oriented and process-oriented studies.

Features of translation, one major research area of CTS, are categorized into translation universals and the features of translation in relation to particular language pairs. Translation universals refer to the universal features of translated texts with respect to the source language or the target language (Baker 1993). These features are unique to translated texts and are not affected by the differences of language pairs. The features of translation in relation to language pairs describe the features of translated texts at lexical, syntactic, and textual levels. They embody the differences between the source and target languages, and reflect a translator's choices and compromises. Research on translator style investigates a translator's idiosyncrasies in their choice of lexicons, syntactic structures, punctuation, and discourse structures, and also their choice of translation strategies and methods. Generally, a translator's style is subject to the constraints of such factors as the disparities between the source language and target language cultures, the socio-cultural contexts where a translator is situated, the translator's personality and language style, and their expectations or the norms of the target readership. In order to unveil the social attributes of translation, research on translational norms aims at investigating a variety of norms that influence translation behaviour in certain historical periods. Translational norms—the norms about the correctness of translation as a product and a process—pose constraints on translation activities, and reflect the values and principles of translation in specific societies and historical periods (Hu 2011: 123). Research on translation process, through the analysis of a large number of translated texts and the use of statistical methods, investigates the attributes and features of translation process, and unveils its cognitive factors and operational norms. Research on translator training focuses on the use of corpora in translation assessment, textbook compilation, and translator training.

TCR aims to reveal psychological mechanisms and cognitive regularities specific to translation by investigating the cognitive process of translation. It also aims to construct a translation model with psychological reality. In particular, TCR investigates the comprehension, retrieval, processing, and encoding of information in the source text in an attempt to construct a cognitive model of translation process.

The major areas of TCR include a translator's mental activities in each phase of translation process, a translator's aesthetic mental set, and the impact of cultural psychology on the translator. Research on translation cognition process primarily involves the psychological activities, cognitive processing, and cognition regularities specific to translation process. Research topics include translation unit, the translator's long-term memory, the manner in which a translator's linguistic and extra-linguistic knowledge are stored and represented, the mechanisms involved in the comprehension and reformulation in the translation process, the translation cognition mechanism for comprehension and expression, the processing system of translation cognition, and the organization and retrieval of the translator's bilingual lexicons in the brain. Research on the translator's mental activities focuses on the translator's psychological activities at different phases of the translation process, including the stimulation of the translator's schemata and imagination. Research on the translator's aesthetic psychology investigates factors including the translator's emotions, resonance, intuition, imagination, associations, and aesthetic mental set, as well as creativity in translation, elegance in translation, and translator style. Research on the impact of cultural psychology on the translator focuses on the translator's motive for translation in a certain cultural setting, and the effect of the motive on translation.

Based on the analysis of the research areas of CTS and TCR, it can be argued that they are complementary to each other in many ways. First, both CTS and TCR involve empirical study. In empirical study, a researcher identifies and generalizes the features and patterns specific to a research object based on the evidence or a large amount of data derived through observation or experiments. Through observation and statistics obtained from the analysis of a large number of bilingual or translated texts, CTS explores the nature of translation and the features of translation process. Similarly, TCR investigates the cognitive regularities of translation process through a number of experiments.

Second, both CTS and TCR investigate regularities in bilingual transfer. For CTS, translation universals and features of translation in relation to language pairs are summed up based on the analysis of regularities in bilingual transfer. The analysis of regularities in bilingual transfer allows us to understand translation universals and features of translation in relation to specific language pairs. Translator style—which is manifested in the translator's use of lexicons and syntactic structures in the target language, and the use of translation strategies and methods—essentially consists of regularities in bilingual transfer specific to a translator. Similarly, the operational norm, one of translational norms, is the theoretical generalization based on the analysis of regularities in bilingual transfer.

For TCR, regularity in bilingual transfer constitutes the research objects for its different research areas. Studies on the mechanism for comprehension and reformulation in the translation process and on the processing system of translation cognition are based on the analysis of regularities in bilingual transfer. Understanding such regularities on lexical and syntactic levels allows us to examine how information in the source text is decoded and encoded in the target language, and then to analyse the regularities and features of the cognitive processes of translation. The core concept of research on the translator's mind set or mentality is the translator's psychological schemata and the translator's imagination. The former is an abstract construction stimulated by bilingual transfer, while the latter comprises the images in the translator's mind evoked by the source text. These images have to be expressed in the target language, which involves regularities in bilingual transfer. Research on a translator's aesthetic mental set analyses creativity in translation, as it is the manifestation of aesthetic mental set. For research in this field, different kinds of regularities in bilingual transfer have to be examined. Moreover, research on the psychological impact of national culture on the translator has to be conducted on the basis of the analysis of regularities in bilingual transfer specific to a translator.

Third, a study on translator style is of interest to both CTS and TCR. A number of studies in CTS have attempted to examine translators' idiosyncrasies in the use of lexicons and syntactic structures, and their personal preferences in the choice of translation strategies and methods, based on the analysis of large amounts of linguistic data (Baker 2000; Bosseaux 2004; Winters 2005). Studies on translator style not only shed light on a translator's subjectivity manifested in translation, which facilitates our understanding of a translator's behaviour, but also reveal the impact of personal and social ideologies reflected in a translation. Although research on translator style is not one of the major research foci(focuses) in TCR, it is indispensable to research on the translator's aesthetic mental set and the impact of cultural psychology on the translator. To analyse a translator's aesthetic and psychological factors, it is necessary to probe into the characteristics of the translator's choice of translation strategies and methods, and their preference in the choice of target language lexicons and syntactic structures, which is one of the main concerns of the study of a translator's style. For example, a comparative analysis of the Chinese translations by Liang Shih-chiu and Zhu Shenghao, two well-known translators in China, shows that Zhu prefers the use of reduplicated words, four-character Chinese idioms, and the words that convey characters' emotions, while Liang frequently uses abstract or general words (Hu and Zhu 2008). This difference is largely associated with the translation purposes of the two translators, and it also reflects the impact of the translators' aesthetic and psychological factors on their translations. Zhu Shenghao wishes to popularize

Shakespeare's play among the masses, and the use of these idioms and words serves to make his translations more readily understood by readers. Liang Shih-chiu intends his translations of Shakespeare's plays to arouse the readers' interest in the original, and he thus sticks closely to the original and translates English general and abstract words into Chinese general and abstract words. Studies of the impact of the psychology of the translator primarily investigate the motivation for the translation and the translator's behaviour based on the analysis of the translator's style. Specifically, in order to explore the impact of cultural psychology on the translator, differences caused by different translators' styles—especially differences in the translation of culturally loaded words—can be examined on the basis of a comparative analysis of different translations of the same source text by people from different countries or ethnic groups.

Lastly, the translation process is the subject of research in both CTS and TCR. While CTS investigates the nature of translation based on the analysis of translation products, it pays equal attention to the study of translation process. Using corpus tools, based on the analysis of the features of a translated text (a translation product), a translator's motivation and behaviour in the process of translation can be analysed. Similarly, a comprehensive and in-depth study of the use of linguistic and paralinguistic signs in interpreting can also be conducted by using multimodal interpreting corpora, for the corpora generally include audio and visual information related to an interpreting activity. The features of interpreting process and the translator's psychological state can be analysed through the analysis of pauses, gestures, and facial expressions made by the interpreter. The features of a translated text can be identified in order to describe the general characteristics and features of the translation process by using a translation process corpus that contains data gathered at different translation phases. In Utka (2004), a phases of translation corpus is used to conduct qualitative and quantitative analysis of the features of the translation process and the normalization tendency in translation. For TCR, the translation process is a focal area of study; research in this field involves the study of cognitive processing of the translator in the course of translation. To reconstruct the cognition process in translation, certain tools and equipment, such as eye tracking technology and magnetic resonance imaging, are used to identify the translator's mental activities and psychological constructs, or their cognitive processing of translation. In particular, research on the translator's mental activities includes the mental schemata inspired by the source text, the translator's attitude towards the specific content of the source text, and the translator's emotions and imagination aroused by the source text.

3 The Implications of CTS and TCR

As has been mentioned, CTS focuses on translation as a product, while TCR examines translation as a process; however, this does not mean that CTS and TCR have nothing in common, or they are irrelevant to each other in terms of research areas. In fact, they are inter-related and mutually complementary, as they focus on different aspects of translation, since a product is shaped through the process in which it is produced whereas the process defines its product. On the one hand, the research findings of CTS can be applied to TCR, on the other, TCR can be used to provide a theoretical basis for CTS to verify its research findings.

3.1 The Implications of CTS for TCR

In recent years, neuro-imaging techniques, including eye tracking and magnetic resonance imaging, have been applied in the study of linguistic representations in the translator's brain and their mental activities in translation. These techniques are useful in the investigation of translation—related language switching mechanisms and neural mechanisms of translation. Focusing on source language lexicons, or on syntactic structures and their counterparts in the target language, these studies, through an analysis of the correspondence between the source language and the target language at lexical and syntactic levels, investigate the psychological mechanisms and information processing in translation by observing eye movement, fixation time, and brain activities.

The bilingual lexicon or syntactic structure involved in TCR used to be determined by scholars according to their intuition and personal judgement. However, a corpus-based analysis of a large number of bilingual texts allows us to obtain the frequency of the correspondence of bilingual lexicons and sentences more easily, which can be used as the criterion whereby a lexicon or sentence is chosen as the entry point for translation cognition experiments so as to ensure objective and scientific research. For instance, for research on the transfer mechanism of the Chinese translations of English attributive clauses, the entry point or the object of study can be determined based on the frequency of the correspondence between the English attributive clauses and their Chinese counterparts.

Research on the translator's cognitive psychology investigates processing models and strategies employed by the translator, using the think aloud protocols (TAP) approach (Li 2017). The study of a translator's cultural psychology examines the effects that cultural factors have on a translator by carrying out surveys and experiments. Although substantial progress has been made in these areas, the reliability and validity of the results of translation psychology would be significantly improved if it were complemented by a corpus-based approach. Generally, CTS explores translators' cultural psychology based on an analysis of the overall tendency or regularities in the translation of culturally loaded words or other typical lexical items. A corpus-based study of translational norms focuses on the analysis of a translator's choice of translation strategies, such as foreignization and domestication, and their use of a particular translation method in translating specific source language lexical items and syntactic structures. The study of translation strategies and methods helps to reveal a translator's aesthetic psychology, the impact of cultural psychology on a translator, as well as their mind set or mentality when coping with the relationship between the source text and the reader of the target text. It is argued that the use of a corpus in TCR will broaden its scope, since the results of the corpus-based studies of a translator's cultural psychology and translational norms also complement and verify the research on translation psychology. Halverson (2010) points out that only by combined methods of experimental and corpus-based approaches can the cognitive basis of translation be better understood.

Research on cognitive processes in interpreting has always been a focus in TCR. Scholars of interpreting studies have approached the features and regularities of cognitive processes in interpreting from the perspective of working memory and information processing (e.g. Zhang 2011). They also examine the cognition process in interpreting using relevance theory (Xu 2007; Sun 2013). However, given the fact that interpreting is a multimodal oral activity, these studies fail to provide a complete picture of either the interpreting process, or the features of the cognitive process in interpreting, since they tend to use a mono-modal interpreting corpus or examine interpreting notes. Multimodal interpreting corpora would enable scholars in this field to overcome some of the limitations of the current research on cognitive processes in interpreting, where the paralinguistic information—including the interpreter's and other speakers' facial expressions and body language—can also be investigated. This would allow us to reveal the interpreter's inner emotions and mental activities more easily. Moreover, the underlying cognition process in interpreting can be revealed through an analysis of the relationship between verbal and non-verbal symbols. It can thus be concluded that research on multimodal interpreting corpora within the framework of CTS will help reveal the process of interpreting and the patterns of cognitive processes in interpreting.

3.2 The Implications of TCR for CTS

Research on the features of translation has continually drawn enormous attention in academia (e.g. Baker 1996; Hu 2009; Hu and Qing 2009; Hu and Zhu 2008; Huang 2008). It has been argued that features of translation are attributable to a number of factors, including differences between languages and distinctions between the styles of different translators, but certain features of translation, such as simplification, explicitation, normalization and levelling out, can be also analysed from the perspective of translation cognition; for example, in accordance with salience principle of cognitive linguistics and other theories related to translation cognition. Specifically, in terms of translation into Chinese, as argued by Wang (2012), a translator tends to 'highlight' the target audience in translation into Chinese to make the translated text easier to follow by Chinese readers, which may give rise to tendencies towards normalization, simplification, and explicitation in the translation. The tendency towards levelling out can be analysed in light of the theory of prototype category, which argues that a category is composed of a prototype and other members. As the typical representation of a category, a prototype has more properties of the category than any other members. It is therefore the core member of the category. Other members similar to the prototype to varying degrees constitute the members in the peripheral areas. It has been found that a translator tends to choose words or phrases denoting a prototype of a category to make their translations more easily understandable and readable, while avoiding the use of the lexical items or syntactic structures that belong to the peripheral use of the category (Wang 2012).

As mentioned, research on the correspondence between the source language and target language lexicons and syntactic structures is the foundation and starting point for CTS. This is due to its major research areas, such as features of translation, translator's style and translational norms, all being based on the analysis of the correspondence between the source text and the target text. By virtue of corpus technology, we can summarize or generalize the overall tendencies and specific manifestations of the correspondence between the source language and target language lexicons and syntactic structures, based on a comparative analysis of the source text and its target text. However, CTS cannot provide ready answers with regard to the motivation for these tendencies and manifestations. Theories pertaining to TCR can be used as tools for possible explanations. For instance, theory of prototype category can be drawn on to account for the correspondence between the source language and target language lexicons. Worthy of note is that an ability to categorize is one of the fundamental cognitive abilities that human beings have and depend on for survival, although there are differences between the classifications of the world by different nationalities. The categories from different cultures that are fully correspondent only account for a small proportion of all the categories. Similarly, schema theory can also be used to explain the correspondence between the syntactic structures of the source language and target language.

Schema, which refers to the knowledge structure that a person possesses as a subject, is the view and understanding of categories. It can be divided into content schema, linguistic schema, and text schema (Hu et al. 2015: 96). Content schema also includes event schema: an event schema is the basis for the formation of grammatical structures or basic syntactic structures (Langacker 1991) that reflect the most typical combination of the participants in an act or state. In this sense, the correspondence of bilingual sentences can be interpreted as a projection of an event schema. To be specific, the syntactic structure of the target language is the mapping or representation of the event schema that is embodied by the syntactic structure of the source text.

It should be noted that theories and principles of TCR can be used to explain patterns found in CTS as well as to verify hypotheses or conclusions in CTS. The frequency of bilingual lexical correspondence is often investigated in CTS, for example the correspondence between English lexicon 'state' and Chinese lexicon 国家, and the results of these studies, can be verified by an eye tracker experiment, or by studying translation behaviours. Generally, the higher the correspondence frequency between a source language lexical item and its target language counterpart, the shorter the time it takes the subject to process bilingual lexical correspondence in the eye tracker experiment. TAP can be used to verify research findings of the operational norms and translation units in CTS, which is a data gathering method used in various research areas in which the subject is asked to verbalize their thought processes as they are undertaking a specific task. The use of this method allows us to restore a translation process—especially the processing of a translation unit, and the selection of translation strategies and methods—so that operational norms of the translation unit can be analysed. Furthermore, research on the contributive factors for a translator's style corroborates the findings on the translator's aesthetic psychology and cultural psychology. Hou's research (2010) shows that a translator's cultural psychology has impacted their style in translating English taboos in Shakespeare's plays. It is argued that the contributive factors for a translator's style include their personal ideology, and the social ideology comprising a translator's aesthetic psychology and cultural psychology. Small wonder that research on a translator's aesthetic psychology and their national cultural psychology, two of the contributive factors for a translator's style, can verify the conclusion with regard to a translator's style in CTS, for a translator's aesthetic psychology and national cultural psychology are generally revealed by the patterns in the use of target language lexical items and syntactic structures, which can be observed by using corpus methodology.

4 Convergence of CTS and TCR: Corpus-based Study of Translation Cognition

It can therefore be argued that CTS and TCR are closely related and complementary. On the one hand, TCR research tends to be subjective, since the researcher in this field generally chooses a lexical item or syntactic structure as the research object based on their intuition and introspection. Its convergence with CTS will thus make it more objective. On the other hand, the convergence of CTS and TCR is a natural and inevitable result of the development of TCR. It is known that a linguistic analysis is an indispensable part of TCR. To achieve satisfactory reliability and validity of the findings, an argument should be made based on the analysis of authentic bilingual data, which can be supported by the corpus-based methodology. In addition, TCR aims to unveil the translator's mental activities in relation to the features of translated texts or the features of translation activities from a cognitive perspective through the analysis of authentic translated texts. In fact, it is precisely because of the above-mentioned relationship that CTS and TCR will finally converge and give birth to a new field of translation studies, which now can be called 'corpus-based translation cognition research' (CTCR).

The aim of CTCR, through using a corpus as a powerful tool, would be to examine the psychological mechanisms and cognitive regularities of translation based on the analysis of a large number of bilingual texts or translated texts. Essentially, CTCR is the result of the mutual influence and integration of CTS and TCR. CTS provides a research methodology for CTCR, while TCR offers a theoretical basis for CTCR. CTCR would primarily involve studies on translation and metaphor, the cognitive processes of translation, the translator's aesthetic psychology, and the impact of cultural psychology on a translator.

The corpus-based study of translation and metaphor analyses the translation of the source language metaphors in the target language, and the cognitive processes and mechanisms implicated in the translation. With the lexical items of the source domains of conceptual metaphors as search items, the source language sentences containing these lexical items and their translations can be retrieved and analysed, on the basis of which we can investigate the reproduction and mutation of the metaphor of the source text in the target language, and the cognitive mechanism behind it. It can also analyse the influence of metaphors in the target language on the translator's expression at textual, cognitive, and discourse levels.

Research on the cognitive process in translation usually adopts a TAP method or eye tracking technology, but a corpus-based approach complements the study in this area; for example, through the use of a translation process corpus or a multimodal interpreting corpus in the analysis of the characteristics and laws of a cognition process in translation. Moreover, the use of a corpus enables us to analyse the translator's choice of translation strategies and translation methods, as well as their choice of a lexical item or syntactic structure, mood, or connotation, based on the analysis of a large number of instances.

A corpus-based study of a translator's aesthetic psychology focuses on the analysis of the translator's aesthetic psychology during the bilingual transfer, including their emotion, imagination, and aesthetic mental set. In general, the translator's emotion is reflected in whether or not the translator, in the process of bilingual transfer, adds emotions that are not present in the original text; the translator's imagination is represented by the use of imagery words in the target language, while the translator's aesthetic mental set can be revealed by the aesthetic properties of the translation. To investigate a translator's aesthetic psychology, a corpus can also be used to analyse the application of discourse markers, modal auxiliaries, evaluative adjectives, and imagery words in the target language, and examine a translator's choice of syntactic structures, rhythms, and rhetorical devices, as well as the structure of the discourse.

Research on the impact of cultural psychology on a translator focuses on the translator's different responses to the same source text, including the translator's motivation in a particular cultural environment and its impact on their translation behaviour, such as the application of different translation strategies and methods, which can be examined by using a corpus.

It can be argued that the birth of CTCR not only broadens the scope of CTS, but also promotes related studies in TCR. First, CTS, since its advent in the 1990s, has focused on translation products or translated texts but has ignored the study of the translation process or translation cognition. However, CTCR can add to the research of CTS in areas of metaphor, cognition processes in translation, and the translator's aesthetic psychology and cultural psychology. Second, the use of a corpus methodology in TCR can help us identify the features of typical lexicons and syntactic structures that cannot be detected with the naked human eye.

5 Conclusion

This chapter, based on an analysis of major research areas of CTS and TCR, has discussed the similarity between CTS and TCR, and the convergence of the two research fields. It has been argued that CTS and TCR are closely related and mutually complementary. As a result, CTS and TCR will converge to give birth to a new field of translation studies: CTCR. CTCR will not only broaden the scope of CTS, but also enrich TCR. However, there is a long way to go before CTCR grows into a fully fledged branch of translation studies.

References

Alves, F., & Vale, D. (2011). On Drafting and Revision in Translation: A Corpus Linguistics Oriented Analysis of Translation Process Data. *TC3: Translation: Computation Corpora, Cognition, 1*, 105–122.

Baker, M. (1993). Corpus Linguistics and Translation Studies: Implications and Applications. In M. Baker, G. Francis, & E. Tognini-Bonelli (Eds.), *Text and Technology: In Honor of John Sinclair*. Amsterdam: John Benjamins.

Baker, M. (1996). Corpus-Based Translation Studies the Challenges That Lie Ahead. In H. Somers (Ed.), *Terminology, LSP and Translation: Studies in Language Engineering in Honor of Juan C. Sager*. Amsterdam: John Benjamins.

Baker, M. (2000). Towards a Methodology for Investigating the Style of a Literary Translator. *Target, 2,* 241–266.

Bosseaux, C. (2004). Point of View in Translation: A Corpus-Based Study of French Translations of Virginia Woolf's *To the Lighthouse*. *Across Languages and Cultures, 1,* 107–122.

Halverson, S. L. (2010). Cognitive Translation Studies: Developments in Theory and Method. In G. M. Shreve & E. Angelone (Eds.), *Translation and Cognition* (pp. 349–369). Amsterdam: John Benjamins.

Hou, Y. (2010). *A Corpus-Based Study of the Chinese Translations of Sensitive Words in Shakespeare's Plays* (Shanghai Jiao Tong University BA thesis), Shanghai.

Hu, K. (2009). Corpus-Based Study of BA-Construction in the Chinese Versions of *Hamlet* by Shakespeare. *Foreign Language Research, 1,* 111–115.

Hu, K. (2011). *Introduction to Corpus-Based Translation Studies*. Shanghai: Shanghai Jiao Tong University Press.

Hu, K., Pan, F., & Li, X. (2015). *Chinese-English Conference Interpreting: A Corpus-Based Study*. Beijing: Foreign Language Teaching and Research Press.

Hu, K., & Qing, T. (2009). Explicitation in the Chinese-English Conference Interpreting and Its Motivation: A Study Based on Parallel Corpus. *Journal of PLA University of Foreign Languages, 4,* 67–73.

Hu, K., & Zhu, Y. (2008). A Corpus-Based Study of Explicitation and Its Motivation in Two Chinese Versions of Shakespeare's *Hamlet*. *Foreign Languages Research, 2,* 72–80.

Huang, L. (2008). Explicitation of Personal Pronoun Subjects in English-Chinese Translation: A Corpus-Based Investigation. *Foreign Language Teaching and Research, 6,* 454–459.

Kruger, A. (2002). Corpus-Based Translation Research: Its Development and Implications for General, Literary and Bible Translation. *Acta Theologica Supplementum, 2,* 70–106.

Langacker, R. W. (1991). *Foundations of Cognitive Grammar: Theoretical Prerequisites*. Stanford: Stanford University Press.

Laviosa, S. (2002). *Corpus-Based Translation Studies: Theory, Findings, Applications*. Amsterdam: Rodopi.

Li, D. (2017). Translation Cognitive Process Research: Evolution and Research Methodology. *Foreign Languages in China, 4,* 10–13.

Olohan, M. (2004). *Introducing Corpora in Translation Studies*. London and New York: Routledge.

Sun, L. (2013). A Study of the Cognitive Processes and Teaching of Interpreting from the Perspective of Relevance Theory. *Foreign Language World, 1*, 79–87.

Utka, A. (2004). Phases of Translation Corpus: Compilation and Analysis. *International Journal of Corpus Linguistics, 9*(2), 195–224.

Wang, K. (2004). *Bilingual Parallel Corpus: Research and Application*. Beijing: Foreign Language Teaching and Research Press.

Wang, K. (2011). *Exploring Corpus-Based Translation Studies*. Shanghai: Shanghai Jiao Tong University Press.

Wang, Y. (2012). Cognitive Translatology. *Chinese Translators Journal, 4*, 17–23.

Winters, M. A. (2005). *Corpus-Based Study of Translator's Style: Oeser's and Orth-Guttmann's German Translations of F. Scott Fitzgerald's The Beautiful and Damned* (Doctoral dissertation). Dublin City University.

Xu, M. (2007). Research on the Psychology of Interpreting Cognition Studies. *Journal of Tianjin Foreign Studies University, 6*, 69–73.

Zhang, W. (2011). *Interpreting Cognition Studies: Simultaneous Interpretation and Working Memory*. Beijing: Foreign Language Teaching and Research Press.

Index

K. Hu and K. H. Kim (eds.), *Corpus-based Translation and Interpreting Studies in Chinese Contexts*, Palgrave Studies in Translating and Interpreting,
https://doi.org/10.1007/978-3-030-21440-1